VICKSBURG:
Southern City Under Siege

VICKSBURG
The Warren County Courthouse

VICKSBURG:
Southern City Under Siege

William Lovelace Foster's Letter
Describing the Defense and Surrender of the
Confederate Fortress on the Mississippi

Edited with an introduction by
Kenneth Trist Urquhart

Published by
THE HISTORIC NEW ORLEANS COLLECTION
New Orleans, Louisiana

Cover: "The Federal Army, under General
Grant, Taking Formal Possession of
Vicksburg, July 4th, 1863, After the
Surrender," from a sketch by Francis B.
Schell. 1863. *The Soldier in Our Civil War*
(New York, 1885). Courtesy the New Orleans
Public Library.

International Standard Book Number: 0-917860-12-8
Library of Congress Catalog Card Number: 80-84685
The Historic New Orleans Collection, New Orleans 70130
© 1980 by The Historic New Orleans Collection
All rights reserved
Fifth Printing. Paperback Edition, 1000 copies, 1997
Printed in the United States of America.

Dedicated
to the memory of
Lucille Leisure
Great Great Granddaughter of
William Lovelace Foster

CONTENTS

ACKNOWLEDGMENTS

The editor of this work is indebted to many people for their assistance in bringing the Reverend William Lovelace Foster's letter to press. He shall never be able to thank adequately three ladies: his wife, Mary Virginia Urquhart; Catherine C. Kahn of the Manuscripts Division of The Historic New Orleans Collection; and Marie A. Kambur, former Assistant Librarian of The Collection, for the seemingly endless hours which they patiently devoted to assisting him in editing the Foster letter. From retracing the Confederate chaplain's steps across the battlefield of Vicksburg, to typing, researching, and puzzling over difficult words, written in haste in an awkward and much faded hand, their intelligence, humor, and encouragement have been invaluable. Although he is unable to mention everyone by name in a brief acknowledgement, he would be remiss in failing to express his appreciation to Inez Harrison, for photocopying and other valuable assistance; to Florence Jumonville, Librarian, for proofreading and typing the manuscript; and to Susan Cole, Manuscripts Curator, for preparing the bibliography, and taking on many of Cathy Kahn's duties while she assisted the editor. Dode Platou, Chief Curator, John A. Mahé II, Curator, Rosanne McCaffrey, Curator, and John H. Lawrence, Associate Curator, were very helpful in assisting in locating suitable pictorial material, and in helping to design and prepare the layout of this work. The editor is especially grateful to the members of the Board of Directors of The Historic New Orleans Collection for allowing the publication of this historic document, a highly prized holding of The Collection. A special word of thanks is due the family of Edwin Blair, grandson of Rev. William L. Foster, for generously making available to The Historic New Orleans Collection the original manuscript of the

Foster letter and related materials, which were invaluable in editing the Letter and in writing the Introduction. The editor is indebted to the Director of The Collection, Stanton Frazar, for prodding him on to publication and for his encouragement and assistance in many ways. He is also indebted to Dr. Robert Bush, Assistant Director and Head of Research, and to his other colleagues at The Collection for their encouragement and help.

The editor gratefully acknowledges the kindness of Dr. William Stanley Hoole, former University Librarian of the University of Alabama, who had planned to publish Rev. William L. Foster's letter, but, upon learning of its acquisition and projected publication by The Historic New Orleans Collection, very generously gave his file of research material on Foster to the editor. Several other individuals and institutions deserve to be acknowledged for the assistance which they rendered: Gordon A. Cotton, Director, Old Court House Museum, Vicksburg; the staff of the Vicksburg National Military Park; Elizabeth C. Wells, Special Collection Librarian, Samford University, Birmingham, Alabama; the staff of the Mississippi Department of Archives and History, Jackson, Mississippi; and Mike Music, Research Consultant, and the other members of the staff of the National Archives, Washington, D.C.

Special thanks go to Christian Urquhart, who was most helpful in the final stages of preparing the manuscript for the press.

INTRODUCTION

On December 20, 1860, decades of bitter rivalry between the Northern and Southern states culminated in the secession of South Carolina from the Union, triggered by the election of Abraham Lincoln to the presidency of the United States in November. The Union was dissolved! In early January, Mississippi became the second state to leave the Union, followed immediately by Florida and Alabama. By February 1, Georgia, Louisiana, and Texas, the other states of the Lower South, had joined their neighbors in secession. These states sent delegates to a convention in Montgomery, Alabama, in February, 1861; organized the Confederate States of America; and elected Jefferson Davis of Mississippi Provisional President of the new nation. Less than four months after South Carolina left the Union, the Civil War began when Confederate cannon bombarded the United States garrison occupying Fort Sumter in Charleston harbor on April 12, 1861. Thus it was that the neighboring states of Mississippi and Alabama severed their ties with the United States; joined the Southern Confederacy; and shortly thereafter became involved in a war, the devastating magnitude of which no one, in the spring of 1861, could possibly have envisioned.

Closely watching the momentous steps being taken by Mississippi and Alabama was a young Baptist preacher, William Lovelace Foster, a native of Alabama, who had moved from that state four years before, in order to minister to congregations in Mississippi. The Reverend Mr. Foster was living in Starkville when the Civil War broke out. The capture of Fort Sumter by the Confederates caused President Lincoln to call for 75,000 volunteers, to increase the size of the United States army for the purpose of forcing the seceded states back into the Union. President Davis of the Confederacy responded by calling for Southern volunteers in order to expand the newly created Confederate army so that it would be able to defend the South against impending Northern aggression. In July, 1861, the first major battle of the war was fought at Bull Run, near Manassas in northern Virginia, where the Confederates achieved a significant victory, largely through the use of units raised in response to President Davis's call for volunteers. The Confederate victory at Manassas and the continued refusal of the United States government to recognize the new Confederacy stimulated the formation of additional volunteer units which were rapidly mustered into the Confederate army. Extensive Southern volunteering continued well into the summer of 1862. Men from all levels of society and every calling in life enlisted in Confederate units to defend their homeland from attack. Among those who responded to the call was Foster, who enlisted in the 35th Mississippi Volunteer Infantry Regiment on May 1, 1862. When he volunteered, although he was a college graduate and a Baptist preacher, he enlisted as an ordinary private in the ranks, because the position of chaplain of the regiment had already been filled by another minister.

Shortly after Foster joined the 35th Mississippi, his regiment entered the Confederate service, becoming part of Brigadier General John C. Moore's Brigade of the Army of Mississippi. By September, 1862, the 35th and the other regiments of Moore's Brigade were serving in northern Mississippi near Tupelo. Early in the following month, the 35th had its first real experience of active warfare when it participated in the Battle of Corinth, Mississippi, where it "acted nobly and did good service," participating in a desperate charge upon the enemy's works during which Moore's Brigade sustained heavy casualties. After Corinth, the 35th Mississippi continued to serve under General Moore, ultimately joining the forces assigned to defend Vicksburg, the most important Confederate stronghold on the Mississippi River.

At the time when Foster had enlisted in the 35th Mississippi Volunteers, developments of far-reaching conse-

quence were taking place in the western Confederacy. Not long after the war began, the Union high command had established the conquest of the Mississippi River as of top priority in its strategy for the defeat of the Confederacy. The great river divided the Confederacy into two parts of almost equal size, and control of it by the Union would effect the severing of Louisiana, Arkansas, and Texas, rich in supplies and recruits, from the Confederate armies fighting in the east. Control of the river would also allow uninterrupted passage of Union ships, troops, and supplies to New Orleans and the Gulf of Mexico. On the other hand, loss of the river would effectively cut the Confederacy in two, severely damage Confederate morale, and greatly hamper Southern efforts to gain diplomatic recognition by European nations. Thus, almost from the day the war began, conquest of the Mississippi River was an essential facet of Union strategy.

It took some time for the Union government to put its strategy for the conquest of the Mississippi River into effect; but by early 1862, Northern forces were prepared to move against Confederate posts on the river. The Union attack came from two directions—Kentucky on the north and the Gulf of Mexico on the south. In February, 1862, Columbus, Kentucky, the Confederate bastion on the Mississippi, was rendered untenable by Union successes in northwestern Tennessee. Columbus was ordered evacuated; and by March 1, the last Confederate units had withdrawn to Island Number 10, near the Kentucky-Tennessee border. A successful Union attack on Island Number 10 forced the surrender of that position on April 8, pushing the Confederate defense of the Mississippi River southward to Fort Pillow, the last defense on the Mississippi north of the important Southern riverport of Memphis, Tennessee.

While Northern forces were gaining control of the Mississippi River in Kentucky and Tennessee, another Union force, led by Flag Officer David G. Farragut, moved from its staging area at Ship Island on the Mississippi Gulf Coast; entered the mouth of the river; and, after being delayed several days by heavy fire from Forts Jackson and St. Philip, captured New Orleans, the Confederacy's largest city, on

April 25, 1862. Three days later Forts Jackson and St. Philip surrendered. The Mississippi from the Gulf of Mexico to New Orleans was now controlled by the Union; and United States troops under Major General Benjamin F. Butler were able to occupy New Orleans without difficulty on May 1, 1862.

Union conquest of the Mississippi above New Orleans moved swiftly. By mid-May, Baton Rouge, Louisiana, and Natchez, Mississippi, had been captured; and on May 18, a Union fleet arrived at Vicksburg, Mississippi. Situated on a high bluff above the river, Vicksburg did not present the same easy target for guns of the Union fleet as had low-lying New Orleans. The Union navy, which thus far had carried all before it, confidently demanded the surrender of the city. Brigadier General M. L. Smith, Confederate officer in charge of the defense, was now busily engaged in strengthening the city's fortifications, and refused to surrender. He was supported by Vicksburg's mayor and by the commander of the Vicksburg post, who informed the commander of the Union ships that ''Mississippians don't know, and refuse to learn, how to surrender to any enemy.'' The Union ships responded by firing on the city; but they were unable to compel it to surrender. Vicksburg thus became the major stumbling block for the Union on the lower Mississippi.

Although the Union movement up the Mississippi had been halted at Vicksburg on May 18, 1862, the Union movement down the river, having delayed for several weeks at Fort Pillow, got under way again with the capture of Memphis, June 6. The Union advance continued southward until the southbound fleet arrived before Vicksburg on July 1, 1862. Here it encountered Farragut's fleet at anchor just north of the city. Farragut had succeeded in getting past the Vicksburg batteries three days before. While passing the city, Farragut's fleet had subjected Vicksburg to a heavy bombardment in the hope of forcing the city's surrender. Vicksburg stood firm, however. Not only did it refuse to surrender; but it withstood all subsequent bombardments; and its defenses were strengthed by the addition of the Confederate ironclad *Arkansas*. It soon became evident to Farragut that Vicksburg could be captured only by a large land force. Since there was no prospect of such a force arriving soon, and as conditions on the river during the hot summer months became increasingly unfavorable, the two Union fleets withdrew from Vicksburg late in July.

Vicksburg, with its massive firepower, could not be ignored. As long as the Confederates held it, Union shipping could not move freely on the Mississippi; and Confederate communications, supplies, and reinforcements had a protected route for crossing the river. Vicksburg's already formidable strategic importance was enhanced in early August when Port Hudson, 250 miles by river to the south, was occupied by Confederate troops who developed there a heavily fortified position on the bluffs overlooking the Mississippi. Now a significant stretch of the river, with Vicksburg on the northern end and Port Hudson on the southern, was held once again by the Confederates. Union success in the Civil War required that Vicksburg be captured from the Confederates. President Lincoln believed it was "the key." "The war can never be brought to a close," he declared, "until that key is in our pocket."

Of prime importance to Lincoln at this point in the Civil War was placing a general in command of the Union forces on the Mississippi who was capable of capturing Vicksburg from the Confederates. In October, 1862, Lincoln appointed Major General Ulysses S. Grant commander of the Department of the Tennessee, with specific instructions to capture Vicksburg and to clear the Mississippi River of any Confederate forces which might pose a threat to Union success in the war. Grant promptly went to work on his new assignment.

In December, 1862, he led an expedition southward from Memphis with the object of placing his army east of Vicksburg in order to strike the city in the rear where it was most vulnerable. He was forced to terminate this expedition when Confederate cavalry succeeded in destroying his supply base. A concurrent expedition which Grant sent down the Mississippi under Major General William T. Sherman was able to reach a point a few miles north of Vicksburg; but

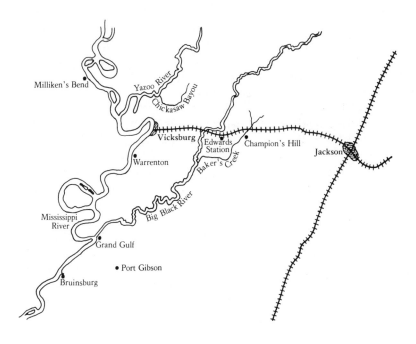

GRANT'S VICKSBURG CAMPAIGN
March - July 1863

Sherman's troops were forced to withdraw when they were repulsed by Confederate forces at Chickasaw Bayou on December 29, 1862.

During the early months of 1863, expeditions which Grant sent along various rivers and bayous failed because of the rugged terrain around Vicksburg. Grant's attempt to dig a canal across the river bend opposite Vicksburg was equally unsuccessful. Critics in the North argued that he was a failure and cried out for his removal. President Lincoln refused, saying that he would like to try Grant a little longer.

Toward the end of March, 1863, Grant embarked upon a bold campaign which would ultimately lead him to success. On March 29, the Union army set out from its camp at Milliken's Bend, 20 miles northwest of Vicksburg, moving southward through Louisiana. Its destination was a point on the Louisiana side of the Mississippi opposite Grand Gulf, 25 miles south of Vicksburg. Grant's army moved slowly over poor roads, often having to cross streams and terrain covered with flood water. There was little Confederate opposition, and the Union forces were able to reach their destination by the last week of April. In the meantime, Union gunboats and transports, carrying much needed supplies, succeeded in running past Vicksburg batteries; and joined Grant's army below the city. After bombarding the Confederate fortifications at Grand Gulf, the Union boats moved a few miles to the south, and, on April 30, 1863, ferried Grant's army across the Mississippi to Bruinsburg, Mississippi.

There was no immediate opposition from the Confederates, and the Union army was able to move rapidly inland toward the town of Port Gibson. Here, on May 1, a small Confederate force attempted to check the Union advance, but was defeated by Grant's numerically superior forces. The Union army then moved toward the northeast, heading for the railroad line connecting Vicksburg and Jackson, the latter an important Southern rail center and capital of the state of Mississippi. Learning that Lieutenant General John

C. Pemberton, with the bulk of the Confederate army from Vicksburg, was near the rail line to the west of the advancing Union army, and that General Joseph E. Johnston, newly assigned commander of the Confederate forces in Mississippi, was in Jackson to its east, Grant decided to strike Johnston before he could organize a force sufficiently large to assist Pemberton. Johnston, realizing that his forces were insufficient to defend Jackson, withdrew to the north. The Union army occupied the city on May 14. Grant then immediately turned to the west to attack Pemberton's army standing between him and Vicksburg. The Union army advanced rapidly from Jackson, and encountered the Confederate army at Champion's Hill, near Baker's Creek, on May 16, 1863.

After unsuccessfully attempting to stop Grant's advance at Champion's Hill and the Big Black River, Pemberton withdrew his forces into the Vicksburg defenses. Here his men were in a better position to withstand the powerful Union army. The Vicksburg fortifications offered excellent protection; and the Confederate garrison of the city provided fresh troops to assist Pemberton's battle-weary soldiers. Among the Confederate units garrisoning Vicksburg when Pemberton arrived, which were now part of his army preparing to defend the city, was the 35th Mississippi Infantry Regiment of Moore's Brigade, of which William Lovelace Foster was a member. Recently promoted to the position of regimental chaplain of the 35th, it was in this capacity that Foster served during the siege of Vicksburg.

Pemberton's troops had hardly gotten into position before units of Grant's advancing army began to close in on the city. By noon of May 19, Grant's forces had surrounded Vicksburg. He immediately ordered a general assault, hoping to take Pemberton's demoralized army by storm. Much to Grant's chagrin, his troops were repulsed in ferocious fighting by Confederate units which had not lost the will to fight. A second and more determined attack was made on the Confederate fortifications on May 22; but again the Union troops were thrown back with heavy losses. At this point, Grant decided to move more slowly against Vicksburg,

VICKSBURG DURING THE SIEGE
"Union troops repulsed in ferocious fighting"

expecting that, as his siege became more effective, it would demoralize Pemberton's forces into submission.

The siege of Vicksburg, which began in mid-May, lasted an incredible forty-seven days. As it progressed, Foster, conscious of the drama and the tragedy taking place around him and of which he was a part, decided to write his wife a letter describing life as he experienced it in the beleaguered city. He began his letter on June 20, probably using notes which he had kept from an earlier date. He wrote ''at broken intervals of time,'' with many interruptions, ''in the midst of danger,'' when he never knew at what moment he might be killed or severely wounded by a bullet or by an exploding shell. By the time the siege had ended and Vicksburg had surrendered, July 4, 1863, Foster's letter had grown to seventy-nine pages. In it, he described the siege from the vantage point of the ordinary soldier—the enlisted man and junior officer—with whom he associated daily, and to whom he ministered as army chaplain. A good reporter and a perceptive observer of human nature, Foster produced a uniquely interesting eye-witness account of one of the most dramatic events of the Civil War. Describing the horrors of nineteenth-century warfare in realistic detail, revealing much about the good and the bad traits of men subjected to the agonizing torments of a protracted siege, refusing to soften war's grim miseries with any romantic gloss, Foster bore simple and elegant witness to the courage, toughness, and spirit of the men who endured those horrors with a valor seldom equaled in the annals of history.

Although it is highly improbable that Foster would have considered his long letter about the siege of Vicksburg a major accomplishment of his life, posterity has judged otherwise. We are indeed fortunate that a man of his keen insight and sensitivity wrote this letter. ''Art,'' the great American novelist William Faulkner once wrote, ''is the strongest force man has invented or discovered to record the history of his invincible durability and courage beneath disaster and to postulate the validity of that hope.'' William Lovelace Foster's letter stands as a remarkable record of man's invincible durability and courage, and as such it fulfils art's function exceptionally well. Its message is universal, transcending time and place, one which should serve as an inspiration to all who read it. The Historic New Orleans Collection is privileged to be able to publish William Lovelace Foster's letter in this volume as a sincere tribute to the man who wrote it and to the gallant soldiers who performed their duty with such awe-inspiring courage at Vicksburg in the spring and summer of 1863.

Kenneth Trist Urquhart
Head of Manuscripts Division and Library
The Historic New Orleans Collection

BIOGRAPHICAL SKETCH

William Lovelace Foster
1830-1869

William Lovelace Foster was born in Foster's Settlement, eleven miles southwest of Tuscaloosa, Alabama, on January 29, 1830. He was the seventh child of Robert Savidge Foster, a wealthy Alabama planter, and Ann Tompkins. The Foster family had its roots in Virginia where William's father had been born in 1796. His grandfather and his father established a citizen-soldier tradition for their family with his grandfather, John Foster, serving in the American Revolution; and his father serving in the Alabama State Militia, in which he held the rank of Brigadier General. William's father, much interested in education, saw that William and his brothers received a "thorough" education in the schools of their neighborhood, and later at the University of Alabama in Tuscaloosa. William L. Foster entered the University in 1847 and graduated with distinction, receiving his B.A. in 1850. Four years later he received an M.A. from the same institution.

Born of pious Baptist parents, William felt called to the Baptist ministry. He began by preaching under the sanction of Grant's Creek Church in Tuscaloosa County; and was ordained to the full ministry about 1853. Rapidly establishing a reputation as an effective preacher, he accepted an invitation in December, 1855, from Colonel Simeon Maxwell, a highly respected and important land owner of Greene County, Alabama, to preach at the Baptist Church of Clinton. He was so well received by the congregation of the Clinton church that he was selected on January 6, 1856, to be the church's pastor. Six months after becoming pastor at Clinton, Foster married Sarah Mildred Maxwell (1835-1893), daughter of Colonel Maxwell. The wedding took place on July 15, 1856, and shortly after their marriage, the Fosters moved to Clay County, Mississippi, where he became pastor of Siloam, Mayhew Prairie, and other churches near West Point, Mississippi.

Foster was a man of great amiability, personal magnetism, high moral character, and dedication. Early in his ministry, he established the firm principle of never disappointing a congregation by failing to appear at the appointed hour for services, often braving inclement weather and swimming swollen creeks to reach his congregations. His tireless dedication to his calling earned him the deep devotion of the people of his churches.

Not long before the outbreak of the Civil War, the Fosters moved to Starkville, Mississippi, where they were residing, in the spring of 1862, when he enlisted as a private in Company F of the 35th Mississippi Volunteer Infantry Regiment. While still a private in this regiment, he was appointed regimental chaplain, effective February 1, 1863, to fill the vacancy caused by the death of the Reverend F. M. Haynes. His regiment was then serving with the units assigned to the defense of Vicksburg. Foster was present when Vicksburg was besieged by Union Forces under General Grant (May 18-July 4, 1863). While there, he wrote the lengthy letter giving valuable details about the siege and the surrender of the Confederate fortress on the Mississippi River—the letter which is the subject of this publication.

When Vicksburg fell on July 4, 1863, Foster was paroled with the other soliders who were surrendered. He returned to active duty in the Confederate army in the summer of 1864, took part in the Atlanta Campaign, and served faithfully until the end of the war in the spring of 1865.

Returning home, Foster resumed his pastoral work at Siloam, Mayhew Prairie, and other Baptist churches in Mississippi. In the fall of 1866, he resigned his pastoral charges to accept the Professorship of Mathematics at Waco University, now incorporated into Baylor University, Waco, Texas. After six months, however, he gave up his position at the university because he believed that his teaching responsibilities interfered with his primary calling as a minister of God. In September of 1868, William Lovelace Foster became pastor of the Baptist Church in Ladonia, Texas, and died less than a year later, on August 5, 1869. He was thirty-nine years old, a comparatively young man, but, during his brief but eventful career, one who had accomplished much good.

EDITOR'S NOTE

In publishing this transcription of Foster's letter, every effort has been made to remain faithful to the original and to make as few changes as possible. Thus, the spelling and grammar of the original have been retained, even when they are incorrect. Writing under the extremely difficult conditions of the siege of Vicksburg, Foster not surprisingly allowed spelling and grammatical errors to occur in this letter, and omitted a word occasionally. His extremely difficult handwriting and the faded condition of several sections of the original letter render it impossible for the editor to make any absolute assurances that every word has been transcribed as Foster intended it to be read, but the editor is confident that the transcription presented in this volume is, in most instances, accurate and of a sufficiently high standard to meet the needs of historical scholarship. When, in the judgment of the editor, an omitted word should be included, he has placed it in brackets. Where proper names are misspelled, the original spelling has been retained in the text, with the correct spelling given in the notes. The punctuation of the original letter is very unconventional, consisting primarily of dashes, and the editor has found it necessary, in the interest of clarity and readability, to substitute periods, commas, and other appropriate marks of punctuation.

Vicksburg. Miss
June 20 ?

My dear Mildred -

When I wrote you last
told you that the storm was gathering in
West. It was not long before the enemy la
ded at Grand Gulf after considerable resista
took possession of Fort Gibson Gen Bowen
division crossed over Big Black, not far fr
its entrance into the Mississippi River & ende
ored to check the enemy in their progress - a
engagement was brought on - & our forces dr
en back before overwhelming numbers - At t
time our Brigade was stationed about two
centon which is on Pine River eight miles
low Vicksburg. In a few days after Bowens
defeat, some of his troops passed our cam
worn down & exhausted from repeated force
marches. The enemy had been pursuing the
hanging upon their rear, capturing those th
were unwell or too much exhausted to mar
& causing our men to push forward with
all their might. It always makes me fe
sad to behold a retreating army - There
go covered with dust - with a swinging ga
hungry, thirsty, tired, sleepy & discouraged
I heard one remark that he had not sle
any for two nights. The victorious enemy mo
on with exceeding rapidity - They seem t
march straight upon Edwards Depot - A po
tion of their forces take possession of Jack
without a blow - Johnson retiring with a sma

WILLIAM LOVELACE FOSTER'S LETTER

Vicksburg, Miss
June 20 1[863]

My dear Mildred[1]

When I wrote you last, [I] told you that the storm was gathering in the West. It was not long before the enemy landed at Grand Gulf after considerable resistance & took possession of Fort Gibson.[2] Gen. Bowens Division[3] crossed over Big Black, not far from its entrance into the Mississippi River & endeavored to check the enemy in their progress. An engagement was brought on & our forces driven back before overwhelming numbers. At this time our Brigade[4] was stationed about Warrenton which is on the river eight miles below Vicksburg. In a few days after Bowens defeat,[5] some of his troops passed our camps worn down & exhausted from repeated forced marches.[6] The enemy had been pursuing them, hanging upon their rear, capturing those that were unwell or too much exhausted to march & causing our men to push forward with all their might. It always makes me feel sad to behold a retreating army. There they go—covered with dust—with a swinging gait, hungry, thirsty, tired, sleepy & discouraged. I heard one remark that he had not slept any for two nights. The victorious enemy move on with exceeding rapidity. They seemed to march straight on Edwards Depot.[7] A portion of their forces take possession of Jackson[8] without a blow—Johnson[9] retiring with a small /p. 1/ [force]. But they do not stop there, satisfied [with] the capture of the Capitol of the State. [Now] they seek nobler prey. They again unite [the]ir forces & press on for Vicksburg. Steph[ens]on's & Bowen's Divisions[10] together with Lorings,[11] are sent out to meet them beyond

Big Black. Forneys Division[12] are left to garrison V___.[13] On Saturday the 16 of May the Battle of Bakers Creek[14] was fought. Our troops were completely surprised & were nearly surrounded before they knew it. Nearly all of our artillery was captured at a single dash. For a while our men fought bravely. Heavy musketry was carried on for hours in fearful proximity. A Tennessee Regiment gives way—Our lines are broken—The men discover that they are being fast encircled by the enemy—They retire in utter confusion. There is only a small gap through which they can escape, & even there the river presents a considerable obstruction. They throw away their guns & cartridge boxes & plunge into the water. Many drown in attempting to swim across—others are shot while crossing by a close pursuing foe. They take a stand in some entrenchments on the West side of Big Black. The victorious enemy, like a rushing whirlwind, drive them out of the very ditches. They retreat in utter route, broken, shattered & dispirited. What a helpless thing is a defeated army! What an utter wreck of former power & strength! How impossible to recover & /p. 2/ rally! Gen. Lorings Division in endeavoring to cover the retreat is cut off & forced to retire toward Jackson. While this battle was progressing our Brigade was quietly encamped above Warrenton. Our Regt. was protecting a very important Battery on the River. On Sunday morning, the 17 of May we could hear distinctly the artillery on Big Black. For half an hour it was exceeding rapid. Our minds were in deep suspense as to the result. Presently we saw a cloud of black smoke rise up in the distance in the direction of the firing. We knew that it was the railroad bridge across Big Black that was burning. Then for the first time the dark suspicion crossed our minds that we were defeated & compelled to fall back beyond the river & to burn the bridge for as yet we had heard nothing reliable about the result of the battle. The smoke in the distance soon died away & the firing of cannon ceased & all was quiet again. It was now my regular hour to preach. A good congregation soon collected around my tent & I endeavored to preach to them on the shortness of life. It was no doubt

the last sermon that several ever heard. No sooner had
we dismissed the meeting than we received marching
orders. In a few minutes we were on our way to Vicksburg. Lieut. Brack.[15] & myself walked [alo]ng together
talking about our prospects. When we reached a high
commanding point, from /p. 3/ which we could see a large
portion of our brigade moving on in their winding way,
Lieut. B___ remarked "It makes me feel sad to look upon
that army." "Why so", I inquired. "Because", said he,
"those men will soon be disarmed & on their way to
some Northern prison. I rebuked him for his dispondency
& replied, "No Sir, they will soon be shouting victory,
while pursuing a routed foe. It yet remains to be seen
who is the true prophet.

We now approach the lines of our defences around
the rear of Vicksburg. We see the ditches all along filled
with men, having taken their positions and now for the
first time we learn of our sad defeat on Bakers Creek. We
converse with men who were in the fight & they confess
that they were badly beaten. With deep curses some de-
nounced Gen. Pemberton[16] as a traitor & as having sold
the place. A strong & muscular Missourian swore with
flashing eyes & compressed lips & a frowning brow, that
if Pemberton surrendered V— his life would pay the
forfeit. The despondent said, "Vicksburg is gone up—it
will be taken by storm". The hopefull replied, "Let them
attack us in these ditches if they dare". Upon the whole,
the army was discouraged—that is, the portion that had
been engaged. Forneys Division was fresh & bouyant &
hopeful.

The line of defences around Vicksburg began about
one mile & a half above the centre of the /p. 4/ town, extending in crescent form around & ending about two
miles below on the river. Our lines at the most remote
point were not more than a mile & a half from the
river—their whole extent on the outward circumference
not much short of five miles. On either flank there were
two lines. On the centre but one line of defences & this
consisted of a very inferior ditch about four feet wide &

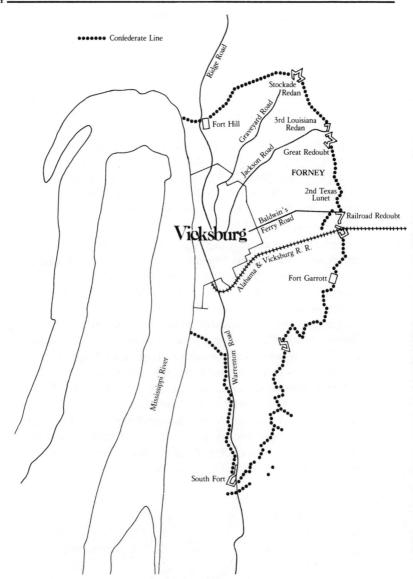

●●●●●● Confederate Line

Ridge Road

Stockade
Redan

Fort Hill

Graveyard Road

3rd Louisiana
Redan

Jackson Road

Great Redoubt

FORNEY

2nd Texas
Lunet

Baldwin's
Ferry Road

Railroad Redoubt

Vicksburg

Alabama & Vicksburg R. R.

Fort Garrott

Mississippi River

Warrenton Road

Fort Garrott

South Fort

THE SIEGE OF VICKSBURG

*"The line of defenses around Vicksburg began about
one mile & a half above the centre of the town,
extending in crescent form around & ending about
two miles on the river."*

as many deep. The places constructed for batteries were strong earthworks, with the usual embrasures—none of them casemated. There were no ditches cut for the purposes of retiring & no obstructions to cut off an enfilading fire.

Behind these works our army consisting of about 20,000 men took their position on Sunday evening, the 17. The question now was "Will the enemy come— "Will they try to take the place by storm. The impression, so far as I could ascertain, was, that the Yankees would not attack us in the ditches. Some thought they would fall back upon Jackson, fortifying that place & then operate against us—by cutting off our supplies. Others thought that they would certainly make an assault & were anxious for them to try it. The despondent expected to see the place carried by storm & thought there was no hope for us. On Sunday[17] night all slept on their arms, opposite their places in the line of battle. On Monday[18] morning the question became still more pressing & interesting, "Will the enemy come" "When will they be here?" /p.5/ During the forenoon flying rumors came in that the enemy had crossed Big Black & were coming rapidly on—that our advanced pickets were driven in. Then came the startling intelligence that Snyders bluff[19] was evacuated & that all our splendid siege pieces had been spiked & fallen into the hands of our victorious foe. Thus the whole Yazoo Valley was in their possession & we could be cut off from supplies in that direction. Besides they could now so easily supply their own army having possession to this valuable inlet to the great River.

On they came, driving in our scouts & pickets. In the evening a canon is heard not far distant on our left. Omenous sound! As the loud clap of thunder gives warning of the coming storm, so does the resounding cannon ever open the fierce battle. A few hours later the distant popping of small arms are heard. This sound becomes nearer & more frequent. Now & then the cannon chimes in. Towards sunset our pickets are driven in near our entrenchments & the enemies sharpshooters advance boldly.

Rapid skirmishing begins on the left & gradually extends around towards the centre. The impudent foe is indeed encircling us. Night comes on but the small arms do not cease. The risky sharpshooter under cover of darkness endeavors to secure a closer position. That night was a solemn night for the soldier. None but /p.6/ those who have had the experience can tell the feeling of the soldiers heart on the night before the approaching battle—when upon the wings of fond imagination his soul visits the loved ones at home—and while he thinks of a lonely & loving wife whose face he may never look upon again & who may never see his form any more on earth, his heart bleeds & dark forebodings fill his mind. Then when he lies down upon the cold ground & looks up to the shining stars above, the gloomy thought crosses his mind, that it may be the last time he will ever look upon the shining heavens & that those same stars which now look down so quiet upon him, may behold him on the morrow night a lifeless, mangled corpse. If he be a child of God, he will commit his soul to God & implore his protection. If a wicked man he will review the past with remorse & the future with dread & will form a weak resolution to do better from that day if God will spare his life through the battle. By the break of day all expect the direful contest. Skirmishing continues all night. The enemy seem impatient for the day to dawn. The day breaks. The bright sun rises calm & bright, but the thundering battle does not open. Soldiers shake off their dread & begin to breathe more freely. The enemy extend their lines still further. All the buildings in front of our lines are fired so as to prevent obstruction to our canon & the enemy from sheltering. /p.7/ Dark columns of smoke rise up to the heavens. The fire and destruction of war is before us. The dark clouds of smoke ascending & the lurid flames, darting almost to the clouds, spread a shade of gloom over the surrounding scene & foreshadows the coming storm.

The surgeons select places for the wounded in the hollows just behind their respective Regiments. Litter Bearers are detailed; & since they are poorly supplied

with litters they begin to construct some out of bark &
poles. Since I regarded my duty to be with the wounded
& dying I remained with our surgeon. There was nothing
more than the usual skirmishing in the forenoon, though
it extended nearly around the entire lines. As noon approached the firing increased in rapidity on the left. On
both sides the artillery opens with considerable fierceness.
''Do the enemy design making a charge upon that point,
becomes an inquiry of most intense interest. Perhaps it is
only a feint to cover an attack elsewhere. What awful
responsibility rest upon the commanding general![20] What
sound judgement & discretion ought he to possess. This
thought deeply impressed my mind as I listened to the increased firing on the left. We had Bowen's shattered division for a reserve. But the question is—At what point
shall they be placed. Before they could reach the real point
of attack, the enemy might break through & all be lost.
The firing on the left /p. 8/ continues to increase in intensity. The canonading subsides & a perfect roar of small
arms breaks forth. A charge! a charge! is whispered along
the lines. When this becomes apparent, a strange uneasi-
ness & dread came over my mind. I confess I feared the
result of the enemies first assault upon our works. They
were flushed with success—ever since they had landed at
Grand Gulf they had been victorious. They had utterly
routed our forces at Baker's Creek. They had stormed
the entrenchments on Big Black, run our men out of the
ditches, & with the fury of a tempest had driven them
like chaff before the whirlwind. They regarded our men as
whipped & looked [on] Vicksburg as already taken. They
were eager to reach forth the hand and seize on the long
desired prize. On the other hand our troops were disheartened by their repeated defeats & dispirited by continual retreating—but more than all had no confidence in
either the head or heart of their commanding general.[21]
Many of them had in their minds already surrendered the
place. Was there not cause then to dread the first shock of
this mighty victorious army—Can our men withstand the
mighty concussion that awaits them. Under cover of a
heavy artillery fire they wind through the valleys until

they come in a short distance of our works. In perfect
order they form in a solid body, six deep. They begin
their advance. They think of their late successes & on
/p. 9/ they rush with flying banners & glittering arms.
Their numerous sharpshooters cover their advance. On
they come. Our cannon pours forth the deadly grape into
their ranks. They fill up the vacant gaps, without pausing
a moment. They come now in startling proximity to our
works. Not a musket yet has been fired by our men.
They have received orders to wait until they can see the
white of their eyes. Not a single head is seen above the
works—except now & then a solitary sentinel, who stands
ready to give the fatal signal. They come now in seventy
yards of our lines. Now a thousand heads rise above.
Above the earthworks, a thousand deadly guns are aimed
& the whole lines are lighted up with a continuous flash
of firearms & every hill seems to be a burning, smoking
volcano. The enemies solid columns reel & totter before
this galling fire—like grass before the moving scythe they
fall. For a while they pause & tremble before this deadly
storm of death, & then in confusion & dismay they fall
back, behind the hills. They again rally & make another
attempt. As before our men reserve their fire. But when
they reach the fatal line the same murderous fire is
poured into their bosoms—The same deadly tempest hurls
them back—defeated, scattered & in utter disorder. Our
Reserve reached the assaulted point in time—but their
service was not required. The musketry during this
charge was most fur-/p. 10/ious. After the enemy retired
& the smoke had been dissipated, an awful scene was
spread before the eyes of our brave men. The hillside was
strewn with the dead & dying. Some had fallen just in
front of our works. Two stands of colors were lying in
thirty steps of our ditches. There the colors lay while the
brave standard bearer lies close by, cold in death. Bravely
did the enemy charge & bravely were they repulsed.
While this charge was being made no doubt many hearts
were lifted to Almighty God that he would defend us &
inspire our brave troops with unyielding courage. For
three hours the musketry was incessant. Towards sunset

it decreased until finally nothing could be heard but the
regular sharpshooting. The sun set quietly in the West—
twilight spread its soft pensive light over the hills, & now
the dark mantle of night covers the earth. Even the skirmishing ceases & the booming cannon is not heard.
Thanks be to the Great Ruler of the Universe, Vicksburg
is still safe. The first great assault has been most successfully repelled—All my fears in reference to taking the
place by storm now vanished.[22] The same quiet stars now
look down from the serene skies. Alas! many eyes that
looked up to them now are darkened by death & shall
never open again until the heavens be no more.

At night it was rumored that the enemy would make
an assault under cover of darkness— /p. 11/ all were commanded [to] be ready at a moments warning, while
pickets were placed in front of our lines. But the night
passed away in stillness—unbroken except by the occa-
sional popping of a rifle.

May 20—As soon as light dawned the concealed
sharpshooter opens fire. During the night they had drawn
nigher & their numbers had increased so that the firing
was rapid & dangerous. Our men were commanded not
to fire [—] only when they had a good opportunity—for
percussion caps were scarce. So that our brave boys had
to lie exposed to continual firing without the privilege of
replying. And they must lie down—for the ditches were
so shallow that they would not protect them while standing
upon their feet. They must lie close in the dust. The
enemies bullets skim the top of the parapet & it is
dangerous to expose any part of the person. Now the
enemy with great caution begins to plant their batteries
off in the distance & to open fire upon our works. They
throw shells all around of breastworks—& they burst
with fury in the midst of our brave troops—mangling
their exposed bodies—& sending many of them to their
long home. Yet there is no help. There they lie exposed
to this galling fire calmly viewing their dangerous situation & in awful suspense listening to the whizzing balls
and rushing shells—& to the more /p. 12/ screams of the

wounded & dying companions. Nothing is more painful—
nothing is more demoralizing than to lie under a galling
fire without the power of replying. It is enough to strike
terror into the bravest heart—almost enough to make
cowards of the bravest men! When rushing to the charge
or engaged in active conflict with the enemy, the stimulus
of action & the engagedness of the mind hide from view
the dread danger that threatens. But while one is lying
under bursting shell—at the mercy of these most terrible
engines of destruction, the mind contemplates the danger
without any stumulus of counteracting influence whatever.
In this most wretched condition our men were now placed.
But they were encouraged with the hope that Gen. Johnson[23] would soon come to their relief. And the report was
circulated that before Wednesday night he would attack
Gen. Grant in the rear. All felt that we were now besieged,

that our only hope was from without. But all were sanguine that we could hold the place until that relief came.

Our Quarters—The Surgeons Quarters, where I remained, was located in the hollow just behind our Regt.,
but it was by no means secure from danger. This valley
was about the right distance to catch the spent minnies &
shell. They would come whizing too near our ears to be
pleasant—and the spent bullets, coming with sufficient
force to kill, would strike so near us that we could reach
out our hand /p. 13/ & pick them up without moving
from our position. As yet, the surgeons had dug no caves
for protection. For the first day our doctor had nothing to
do—But it was not long before there was work enough.
On Wednesday, the 20, while the firing was more severe
than usual in front & a new battery had just opened upon
our position a messenger came running to our surgeon,
calling for some brandy, stating that Capt. Coopwood[24]
was dreadfully wounded & was about to faint from the
loss of blood. Presently the litter bearers came with their
mournful burden. There the Captain lies, mangled &
bleeding & groaning. His leg is most awfully mangled. A
twelve pound rifle shell struck him on the left thigh, in-
flicting a most severe flesh wound, & then passed down
on the same leg tearing off the entire calf. The same fatal
shell had struck a private, removing almost entirely one
hip. The doctors worked & dressed these awful wounds
while I endeavored to remove the dust from their hands
& faces, for they were covered with dirt. An ambulance
soon arrived & they were carried off to our Brigade Hospital. The private died on the way. This was a terrible
blow upon Capt. C. company[25] & fell with stunning effect.
His men felt their great loss & their awful danger.

Second Charge—On Thursday the 21st as soon as
light dawned the usual sharpshooting /p. 14/ began, only
more rapid & nearer & dangerous. The enemy were now
placing their batteries all along the line & the shelling
became every hour more intense & destructive. These
furious missiles would explode over the heads of our brave
men & the broken fragments strike down into the ditches,
killing & wounding them while lying on their faces. Here

comes the litter-bearers again, bearing their groaning burden. Who can it be? A man well advanced in age, who has a grown son in the same company, is severely, & as it proved afterwards, mortally wounded by a shell. A fragment passed through his knee, shattering it all to pieces, while his shoulder was also sorely wounded. The old man bore it with so much patience. You can almost tell when a child of grace is wounded—for they generally bear their pain so meekly without scarcely a word of complaint. His wound is bandaged & he is sent to the Brigade Hospital.

Towards evening heavy canonading was heard upon the right. It seems like a half dozen batteries have opened upon one point. The firing is so unusually rapid & fierce that it begins to attract the attention of the whole line. Now the batteries of the enemy open all along the line, & the sharpshooters increase their fire—But on the right the cannonading is hottest. /p.15/ Will the enemy make another effort to storm our works? The canonading now subsides, but the fire of small arms grows more rapid. And now whole volleys of musketry, with one continual roar breaks forth. Another charge is made. In solid columns the persevering foe presses upon our right, endeavoring once more to force our lines. Our men as before reserve their fire until they approach near & then pour forth a perfect storm of 'Buck & Ball', so that the enemy fall by hundreds. They fill up the broken ranks & press on—but they stagger before the deadly fire. Their men will not advance & turn & fly from certain death—But on one point they concentrate a powerful force. They press with great fury & an Ala. Regt.[26] is driven out of the ditches. The Yankees plant their flag upon our works & send back for reinforcements. They take possession of our works & for two hours hold their position. Volunteers are called for to retake the works. Enough readily respond & they with a single dash & but little loss, drive the enemy from the lost ditches, killing & capturing several. Thus for the second time they have failed in their efforts to storm our works. They become discouraged from their failure & heavy loss, while our men gain confidence.

On Friday the 22 the day opened as usual with the popping of small arms & the /p. 16/ booming of cannon. The enemy had succeeded in planting more batteries & the sharpshooters had gained positions nearer our lines. Their first parallel had now completely encircled us & upon every commanding hill was planted a powerful battery. Having failed in storming our works upon the left & then on our right, we were beginning to think that they would abandon the hope of taking the place by force & would be satisfied in laying siege to the place & in annoying and wearing out our people by continued firing & unceasing watching & exposure—But our persevering foe was not willing to give up such a·glorious undertaking, until he had made another grand effort.[27] So in the course of the forenoon an unusual heavy firing both from the sharpshooters & the artillery was opened along the whole line & continued for about one hour. Our brave men had literally [to] lie cleaving to the dust to avoid the worrying minnies & the bursting shells. While the firing was kept up along the whole line, it seemed to be more intense about the centre. Upon the centre every available battery was turned & the very hills made to tremble with the awful fire. The breastworks were torn down over the heads of our men & many were borne away frightfully wounded. Our cannon that would dare to fire were either dismounted or forced to retire. Now about the centre the enemy cease their artillery firing, while the skirmishers increase theirs. /p. 17/ They are forming for a last desperate charge. They come with short ladders to scale the works where they are precipitous. They stimulate their men by every means possible. They promise every man a reward of land & money that crosses our lines. They form as usual into a column six deep & through the winding valleys & by artificial channels they make their way in a few hundred yards [of] our lines. Now with rapidity they advance— Now our cannon pour the deadly grape upon them—but on they come. Our men as before reserve their fire until they approach near. Now they raise their heads above the works & into the bosoms of the foes crowded ranks pour forth a withering, consuming fire. They fall back in confusion—Again they rally their men & make another

charge. The same storm of death drives them back. They
come the third time but meet the same awful fate. They
fall back in utter confusion & dismay, nor can they be in-
duced to make another effort. Thus ended the last &
most desperate effort the enemy made to carry our works
by force. Their loss was very heavy. The hill side was
strewn with their dead. It so happened that every attempt
made to carry our works fell upon Forneys Division,[28]
which was fresh & had not been in the other engagements.
Our loss was comparatively small—Most /p. 18/ of those
that were killed or wounded were shot in the head. After
this repulse the enemy abandoned all hope of taking the
city by direct assault. Their only chance was the slow
process of starving us out. But we felt confident that
Johnson[29] would come to our relief before this could be
effected. As for myself I regarded the city as safe.

Change of base—Since our baffled foe could not take
the place by force, he now endeavors to annoy our men
by a more severe fire. They plant other batteries still &
their sharpshooters dig trenches still nearer our lines &
make their constant firing more galling still. On the next
day the firing upon & over our Regiment was very severe.
The new batteries opened a cross fire upon our battery &
since they had not acquired the range & overshot the
mark, their shell fell over in the hollow where the Surgeons quarters were. Dr. C[30] & myself were lying side of
the hill when these batteries opened upon us. At first the
shell would explode above us & to either side—But at
every shot they would approach nearer, until our situation
became exceeding perilous. With rushing fury they would
pass in a few feet of our heads & then with crashing
sound explode, hurling the singing fragments in every
direction. Close to the hill side we would /p. 19/ lie, not
knowing but the next fire would take off our heads. Presently one exploded just behind us, covering us all with
smoke & the fumes of sulphur. After the loud crash was
over we heard the deep moans of a man severely wounded.
Who could it be? Was it one of the doctors that was with
us. Upon looking around, in a few steps of us—there we
discovered a soldier shot through & through the body

with a ball from one of those loaded shells, weltering in his blood, hardly able to move. The place was too hot to dress his wound there for the fire was not abated in the least. So he was borne higher up the valley & his wound examined & dressed. Poor fellow. He had come into the valley after a canteen of water & he was shirking from duty by staying for hours on the side of the hill, thinking it was safer than in the trenches. Had he been more faithful, his life might have been saved. The post of duty is the post of safety as well as the post of honor. He was carried to the hospital & lingered for several days before he died. The surgeon now thought about changing his quarters—but could not find a place suitable, while all the valley was more or less exposed. These troublesome batteries ceased after awhile & we had comparative quiet in our quarters. /p. 20/ But we were not allowed to enjoy repose long. Towards evening the same crossfire opened upon us, overshooting our works & ranging up & down our valley. Now they come nearer & nearer. Every man hugs close to the hill side. Some get at the root of large trees. Capt. Nilson our Commissary,[31] rides up hitches his horse about twenty steps in front of us & seeks shelter with us under the hillside. A shell now explodes upon our right, & now close by on our left, now one just behind us—& then another in front. Now they burst above us. How awful the rushing, howling sound of those rifle shells, as they pass with the speed of lightning close to your head & then burst with thundering crash in your very ears. They come like howling demons of destruction, rejoicing in death & carnage. What is poor frail man when opposed to such missiles of war? Can his strength or courage avail him anything? Can he fight against the lightnings of heaven? Can he resist the swift thunderbolt when hurled from the hand of the Almighty? Where may he withstand the mighty missiles of war? What heart is that that quails not in the face of such danger? What face but turns pale in the presence of these bursting furies? Surely the demons of hell could not have invented a more terrible & frightful engine of destruction than these exploding bombs. If all the furies of the lower regions were turned loose upon earth to terrify /p. 21/ & destroy the children of men, they could not with all their screams & howlings & fearful noises equal these terrible machines of death. Now, one of these howling monsters explodes right in our midst, but fortunately a little in front of us. The Captains horse is struck down. He falls upon his haunches pierced through with a piece of shell. His entrails protrude. He groans & moans with pitiful cry & tries in vain to rise. The firing grows hotter & hotter. We hold a counsel as to what is best for us to do. Shall we remain or shall we retire. We conclude it is safest to remain, for we had the shelter of the steep hillside & the valley all around is exposed. But no sooner had we come to this conclusion than a shell burst in our very ears & sent its sulphurous fumes in our nostrils. It seems like to remain was death. A hundred yards below would carry us out of the range, though in walking this distance we would be without any shelter. For one I determined to get out of the range, for I was doing no good there. Others determined to pursue the same course. Leaving our shelter we passed down the valley out of the range of that dreadful crossfire. New batteries opened & the whole valley was filled with minnie balls. Most of the men in reserve had small excavations dug in the sides of the hills, which afforded them great protection. When the /p. 22/ firing ceased the doctors again had a consultation about changing their quarters, for the carriers said it was the most exposed position in the whole valley and when they passed they generally went at full speed. But owing to its convenience to the Reg. & to water, they agreed to remain there & to dig caves for protection. On the same evening I visited the Brigade Hospital where the most of our wounded were carried—and since my business was now with the wounded & dying, I thought I could do more good there than by remaining at our Regimental hospital, for as soon the wounds were dressed they were removed to some Brigade Hospital.

The Wounded—This hospital, which was called Hospital No. 1, was situated about a quarter of a mile behind our lines. The building where the sick remained & where

the cooking was done for all, was located on a high hill, a
beautiful residence. The wounded were placed in tents on
either side in deep hollows. As I entered one of these
valleys a most horid spectacle greeted my eyes. Every tent
was filled with the wounded & the dying. There they lay
poor helpless sufferers some groaning from excessive pain,
others pale & silent through weakness & the loss of blood.
As I approached the Surgeons tent, my eyes fell upon the
bloody table upon which amputations were performed.
Upon it had /p. 23/ just been laid a suffering victim, a
man from our Reg. whose knee had been shattered by a
piece of shell. They were applying chloroform to his
mouth & nose. He now becomes insensible & seems to
rest in sweet sleep. The surgeon whose duty it is to perform the bloody job rolls up his sleeves, takes a drink of
brandy to strengthen his nerves. A tight cord is passed
around the leg—then the gleaming knife cuts through the
flesh all around. A flap of skin & muscle is turned back.
Then with a strong stroke the knife cuts down to the
bone & next the saw with quick stroke completes the job
& the leg is removed. The artery having been tied with a
small cord, the flap is then turned down over the stump
& a few stitches complete the job. The leg is thrown on
the ground, where lay other limbs, hands, fingers, etc.
All this time the poor soldier lies sleeping unconscious of
his loss or pain. He is then borne off to his bunk where
he must lie for weeks upon weeks, unless indeed he be
carried to his grave, which was the case with more than
half upon whom this operation was performed. This was
the first case of amputation that I witnessed & it made a
vivid impression upon my mind. The poor boy did not
get over the influence of the chloroform for that day—in
fact he was stupid & drowsy as long as he lived. He survived for seven or eight days & died. /p. 24/

On passing through the hospital what a heart-rending
spectacle greets the eye. Here we see the horrors of dreadful war! It is not on the field of battle amid the confusion
& clamor of arms, where the sulphurous smoke & the
thundering cannon drowns & hides the cries & mangled
bodies of the dead & wounded victims, but in the solemn

hospitals where the wounded & dying are conveyed that the awful horrors of war are depicted. The first sight that greeted my eyes was most appalling. There lay a man with most frightful countenance, scarcely human so much disfigured he was. His hair, eyebrows & eyelashes singed off & his face blackened & burned to a crisp with powder. His mother could not have recognized him—Every feature was distorted—his eyes were closed & water running from his scalded mouth. He belongs to some battery. The caison had exploded, scattering death & ruin all around. His groans are pitiful & low & plaintive. He can only lie upon his back. There he lies & there he must lie for weeks unless death comes to his relief. Passing along still farther on, without mentioning common wounds, I beheld a youth, not more than seventeen, lying on his back—with eyes and face most uncommonly swollen. A ball had passed just under his eye entering his jaw & lodging there in the bone, which could not be removed. Both of his eyes were closed. Not a groan escaped his lips. With difficulty could he eat or drink. In fact he could subsist only on soup & fluids. He could not chew solid foods. There he lay, day after day & week after week, so meek, so resigned, while not a murmur escaped his lips. He could not change his position. /p.25/

Still further on my attention was arrested by a strong, athletic, noble-looking young man, who was wounded by a minnie ball passing clear through his mighty chest. His chest was heaving & his heart palpitating so as to shake his whole body & his whole frame agitated by this fatal wound. What can manly strength & muscular power avail against such missiles of death! The strong as well as the weak fall helpless victims. There lies another, shot through the jaw—his mouth lies open and his tongue is tied back. Here is another scalped on the top of his head—his jaws are locked & he soon dies with convulsions. Another is wounded in a peculiar way. The ball enters his ear, passes out, goes down through his shoulder, lodging in the vital parts of his body. There are several with their legs amputated, who are destined to lie for weeks in one position, unless indeed as it often happens, they are carried to their last resting place. Here are several with their arms cut—There is one with his whole under-jaw torn off & his shoulder mutilated with a shell. He soon expires. Here is one with his arms & leg both amputated. What would life be to him if he could survive. There is one who has had a pair of screw drivers driven into his jaw & temples. He floods his bed with his blood. Another has had his hand torn all to pieces with a thumb and little finger left. One is pierced through the bowels & suffers a thousand agonies before death comes to his relief. Why should I proceed any further? Every part of the body is pierced. All conceivable wounds are inflicted. /p. 26/ The heart sickens at the sight. Low groans proceed from some of the suffering victims, while others with clenched teeth remain silent. The weather is excessively hot & the flies swarm around the wounded—more numerous where the wound is severest. In a few days the wounds begin to be offensive & horrid! The vile insect finds its way into the wounded part & adds to the pain & terror of the poor sufferers. Nor can this be avoided, unless a nurse were detailed for every man, but there is only one allowed for every eight men. Those that can hold a brush in one hand must use it constantly & those that are helpless must suffer. Never before did I have such an idea of the cruelty & the barbarism of war. The heart sickens at the sight. Poor Capt. Coopwood[32]—his wound was the most awful I have ever seen, his whole leg deprived of nearly all its flesh.

On Saturday[33] there was a shower of rain. I was curious to know whether the enemy would cease firing during the rain. Instead of that they rather increased it, no doubt getting a view of our men as they would arise to adjust their blankets. The harder it rained, the more frequent their fire.

Now it is Sunday morning.[34] On account of a severe cold & sore throat & general weakness through dysentery, I could not preach. But there is no Sabbath quiet here— War knows no Sabbath. I thought of the quiet Sabbaths at home & contrasted them with the noise & din of war that was now raging all around us. I thought, will I ever see those peaceful days again. /p. 27/ Here we were shut in by a powerful foe—prisoners. There was no rest for our brave men, nor did our enemies take any. It was a day of no spiritual comfort to my soul. How unnatural is war!

Thus the first week of the siege had ended.[35] The enemy had made the grand assaults upon our works & had signally failed. Will not Johnson[36] come to our relief before another week is ended? Some of us felt sanguine that he would come. His canon had already been heard in the rear, it was thought. It was rumored that we had only ten days rations of bread. Our only hope was from without & Johnsons name was no doubt repeated thousands of times every passing hour. The rations for our men were sufficient during this week, though not full rations. The men were cheerful. The desponding had gained courage by our successes & the sanguine felt more confident. Even the strong prejudices against Pemberton began to soften down. As for my part, I expected to hear Johnsons cannon thundering in the rear—almost as confidently as I expected to see the rising Sun. I expected to see Grants army sent whirling up the great River & I imagined how pleasant it would be for us to go & examine the enemies works & how happy we would be when free once more & no longer molested by shot and shell. During this week many of the enemy had fell to rise no more. This loss must have been heavy. Also several of our brave men had been sent to their long rest. /p. 28/

Second week—[37] On Monday morning the 25 of May, a flag of truce was sent from our General to the enemy requesting that they would bury their dead, for their dead bodies were becoming very offensive, since some of them had been killed nearly one week & the weather being hot decomposition was very rapid. The enemy did not seem to be very anxious to inter their slain, hence we were under the necessity of making this request. The flag of truce was received & the request granted. Presently the firing began to cease on the centre of the line & gradually extended from right & left until

quiet reigned along the whole line. What a relief! For
nearly for a week our ears had been greeted by the continual sound of small arms & canon. Not a moment in
the day passed but brought with it some report. The stillness seemed unnatural, but was very welcome. Now the
enemy make their appearance, coming out of their trenches
& hiding places. They are as numerous as a swarm of
black-birds in the winter season. They come out as numerous as the ants from a freshly stirred up nest. Some of
them with spades & shovels approach to perform the
solemn work of burying their fallen comrades. They dig
ditches near the dead & then roll the putrid bodies in—
sometimes with a blanket for the winding sheet—sometimes with nothing but the clothing in which they fell. A
little earth is thrown over them & there they are left un-
marked, unknown, to sleep until awakened by the last
trump which we all shall hear in the great Judgment Day.
While /p. 29/ this sad work is going on the enemy & our
men approach near enough to hold conversation. The
Missouri Regiments from each side begin to inquire for
friends & relatives. Old friends, once friends, now meet &
extend the welcome hand. A brother meets a brother—
bound by such ties which no relations in life can sever.
They now meet as deadly enemies arrayed against each
other in fatal strife—but still, born & nursed by the same
fond mother they can but love each other. In another
quarter they try to quiz each other. Says a Yankee 'How
far is Joe Johnson in the rear?' The Confederate replies—
Where is your $300.00 bounty & your sixty days fur-
lough. For it is said that the enemy promised every man
who would break through our lines for the above reward.
Neither side received an answer. Another western man
cries out—'I say I want to borrow some coffee & pay
back when Johnson comes up in the rear.' The Confederates make no answer to this cruel taunt, for no coffee
has passed their lips for months & they feel that Gen.
Johnson may not come to their relief soon. The enemy
are not allowed to come up to our works, but are kept back
at a distance sufficient to prevent them from over-looking

"*Now the enemy make their appearance, coming out of
their trenches & hiding places. . . . Some of them with
spades & shovels approach to perform the solemn work
of burying their fallen comrades.*"

our fortifications. The most of the day was thus occupied. The time at length arrived at which the truce expired. Back to your trenches now men! Get down now from the high hills & exposed places. To your guns ye persevering & unrelenting sharpshooters. Separate now ye brothers & relatives & old friends & resume the miserable /p. 30/ work of killing each other. Ye artilerists of the enemy go now to your guns that have now for the first time have grown cold during the daytime in the past week. The storm is now coming—the storm of death—the cruel & bloody tempest of war. Let all seek shelter from the missiles of death. The whole line is now cleared—not an enemy is to be seen. Our brave men lie low in the trenches. The crack of the sharpshooters rifle breaks the stillness— another & another. The firing extends along the line. The booming canon break forth once more. The firing increases—The whistling minnie—the rushing cannon ball & the bursting shell proclaim that the work has again begun. Our ears are greeted with the same old sound & the same suspense & disagreeable emotions fill our minds. Night again comes on & the firing ceases except the booming of a canon occasionally or when some wakeful sharpshooter fires at some dusky object in the distance as a pastime for the weary & lonesome watches of the night.

The Bombardment—The persevering foe now gives up all hope of carrying our works by assault. As yet there had been no firing from the river in the rear upon the city. The stillness & serenity of the twilight is now broken by an unusual sound. A dull heavy sound falls upon the ear. Every ear is directed now to the rear. Now a tremendous explosion takes place high above our heads. It is a mortar shell! The wide-throated mortar has opened upon us. In quick succession another /p. 31/ follows & then another. The air is filled with them. Several mortar boats[38] within easy range now shell the devoted city of hills. They cannot possess the place, so they will endeavor to destroy it. Heretofore the women & children had been safe in their houses—Now no place is secure in the town—houses are no protection from these mighty monsters of death. Now

*"The stillness & serenity of the twilight is now broken
...a tremendous explosion takes place high above our
heads. It is a mortar shell! The wide-throated mortar
has opened upon us."*

there is confusion & bustle amongst the citizens of Vicksburg. There is hurrying to & fro with the women & in-
nocent children. They must leave their comfortable houses
& go to their dark gloomy caves. Better to live in a cave
than to be slain in a fine house. Most of them have caves
in the steep hillsides,[39] which they dug during the long
bombardment to which the city was previously subjected.
In these gloomy caves must they retire for security. The
enemy envy us of our quiet nights & by the time the firing
in our front begins to subside, they open upon us their
mortars to drive away sleep from our eyes & disturb our
repose. These large mortar shells, thirteen inches in
diameter & weighing about two hundred pounds, are sent
clear across the peninsula & reach nearly to our lines in
the rear, passing over a distance of four miles. Within
their range was all our waggon trains, all our hospitals &
even some of our arsenals. Their firing was directed to
different parts of the town. Their fuses were shortened or
lengthened so as to throw them in the heart of the city,
or to throw them in the rear. /p. 32/ The appearance presented by this bombardment at night was grand & terriffic
to the last degree. Directing the eye to the river you first
see a small light about the size of a star, darting like a
meteor through the air, ascending higher & higher in its
progress. This you see before you hear the report, so
much faster does light travel than sound. In a few seconds
you hear a dull heavy report in the distance. The spark of
light, which is caused by the burning of the fuse ascends
higher & higher until it threatens to reach the very stars.
Now it reaches the summit of its orbit & begins to descend
on a curved line towards the earth. Nearer & nearer it
approaches. Now a rushing sound greets your ear, like
the coming tempest when the clouds roar with wind. The
falling star now descends with fearful rapidity & the noise
becomes more furious & terrible. It seems as if it will fall
upon your head. You look with suspense & intense anxiety,
expecting every moment the dreadful explosion. Now it
bursts with tremendous crash & sends its howling fragments singing through the air. They fall all around bearing

ruin & destruction in their path. Another light is seen in the distance. Listen now at the dull sound. See it ascending with almost lightning speed up to the very clouds. Now it begins to descend. Look out! It is coming directly towards us. Hold your breath now—it is about to explode. The storm comes fearfully near. Fall down behind the cliffs & hills & hide from the rushing, falling mountain. It strikes the earth without exploding & shakes the very hills & makes the ground tremble like an earthquake. Instead of falling on our heads it fell a quarter /p. 33/ of a mile distant. All night long they continue their bombardment. The Hospital at which our wounded were carried, was in full range of these mortar shells—also in reach of the minnie balls & canon shot from the lines. But it was convenient & all parts of the town were more or less exposed —the deep hollows afforded some protection.

On the 27 an unusual heavy canonading was heard on our left. The guns seemed to be of heavier calliber than usual. The firing was most rapid for artillery. It turned out to be a combat between one of their gun-boats & our upper water battery. The gunboat[40] with a full head of steam approached fearlessly & proudly. A shot from our splendid rifle canon told her to halt. But she heeded not the challenge—with a defiant air & open port holes draws up in easy range—turns round her broad side

& makes the bosom of the old Mississippi tremble with the shock of her big guns. To your guns now, Ye Confederate artillerists & punish the insolent foe that dares defy your strength. Our battery accepts the challenge & every gun does its part. With keen & cracking report, peculiar to rifle canon, the voice of our guns can be distinguished from that of the enemies. The waters all around tremble & no doubt the fishes terrifed at the unusual noise & shock, retire far from the field of conflict. The resounding noise rolls up the mighty river & echo takes up the sound & rolls it farther on. The gunboat is enveloped in smoke—a cloud of smoke rests over our batteries. Who shall be the victor? A contest so hot & so furious cannot last long—truly, the boat is sunk. /p. 34/ Soon the batteries will be dismounted. Unless our guns are soon silenced the boat must go down. The boat now trembles before our terrible fire. A fatal shot now passes through a vulnerable part—she totters under the fatal stroke. She turns her course & begins slowly to move off. Our shot pursues her with unrelenting violence. Now she careens to one side—her hull fills with water & slowly she settles down in the water & sinks to the bottom. The friendly waves close over her form—nothing but the chimney & the highest part of the upper deck remains, as marking the spot where the conquered victim was buried. The object of the enemy was to carry our upper battery & then plant guns upon the commanding points & force our lines near the river on the left, For our water battery was exceeding annoying to them & could silence any gun which they planted within range.

To the lines again—But how are matters now progressing on the lines. The enemy baffled in their efforts to storm our works, now turn their attention to planting new batteries. This they do on every hill right in the face of our works. Their sharpshooters approach nearer & nearer—So numerous are their heavy guns—that our batteries are virtually silenced. Only occasionally do they dare open fire—Then they bring down upon themselves the concentrated fire of the enemies surrounding batteries, so that their casons are exploded, the carriages broken to pieces, guns dismounted—besides the increased fire of the sharpshooters, killing our artillerists & compelling our pieces /p. 35/ [to] retire for protection. In fact our artillery was of but little service to us, so superior in number & caliber were the enemies guns. We could not prevent them from approaching nearer—so that they planted their guns in our very faces, just as near as they desired.

Their sharpshooters become more annoying this week. They learned the range of our ditches & killed our men while lying flat in the trenches. One poor fellow in our Regt. was lying down fast asleep, not know[ing] that he would never awake again in this world. A ball pierces his head & without a struggle, or scarcely a motion he dies. Another one wishing to retire to the rear, but thinking it too tedious to go down the trenches & enter the ditch leading out for that purpose & supposing that he can go over the exposed point which is but a few steps without danger, makes the attempt. He pays for his daring —a ball pierces his body & he falls mortally wounded. The dirt is being constantly knocked off from the parapet by minnie balls. Then more shells, that can go anywhere, keep the men in constant dread, for they are continually exploding around & killing & wounding somebody. There they must lie under the scorching sun—without scarcely a breath of air. Day after day they must endure its sultry beams—with only an outspread blanket to keep off the rays, which also excludes the air. There they must endure the drenching showers of rain & lie in the mud day & night. /p. 36/

On a certain morning before day during this week we were aroused from our sleep by the most terriffic canonading that ever greeted my ears. The whole air above us was filled with streaming lights, caused by the burning of fuses & the bursting of shells, more frequent than the lightnings flash on a stormy night almost converted the night into day. The whole air around was constantly filled with solid shot & shell. Over the valley of our hospital it seemed that a hundred were passing every moment. A constant rushing & continual bursting filled the atmosphere. The firing of their artillery was as rapid as brisk skirmishing with small arms. It seems that the enemy were endeavoring to frighten our men out of the ditches. It extended all around the lines. They had now mounted all their guns & they were showing us their power. Those in the trenches lie low & those without hug close the hillsides. Those on the outskirts of the town near the lines creep back deep into their caves & the mother hugs her children close to her side. The shells burst all around our men—flashing in their very faces & filling the air around with the fumes of sulphur. The top of our breastworks are in some places leveled with the ditches & our men become more exposed. Do they leave the ditches? Are they frightened out of the works? Like heroes they stand this appalling fire & bear patiently all the fierce wrath of the enraged enemy. Some have slept their last sleep & live not to see again the sweet light of the day. Several shots fell in the valley amongst the wounded but fortunately no one was hurt. /p. 37/ This heavy firing did not last more than half an hour. It was too frequent to continue long, as the guns would soon become too hot to use. It subsided about the dawn of the day. Then the old mortars chimed in again for it seemed that they had ceased during this severe canonading, but it may have been that the noise of these monsters was only drowned by the heavy firing on the lines.

Here comes the sad ambulance. Within are heard doleful groans. The bottom is bloody with newly shed blood. With great pain to the sufferers, their mangled bodies are borne along to the tent prepared for them. Another ambulance approaches—more wounded. We look with anxiety to see if any of our friends are in the number. Thus it was during nearly every day until our hospital was filled. How our men suffer on those rough ambulances. Some of them were simply small waggons without any springs. Just to think of a wounded man with broken

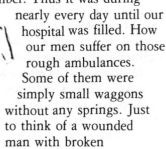

limbs & mangled body being borne on such a rough, jolting vehicle as this. Every step is filled with pain & agony to the poor sufferer. No wonder they groan under such circumstances. It is a wonder that they are as patient as they are.

During this week a great many of our wounded in this hospital died. The first ten days generally decides whether the wound will prove fatal or not. The weather was so warm that many died who might otherwise have recovered. More than one half of the cases in which a leg was amputated proved fatal. /p. 38/ In nearly every case where the leg was broken by a shell death was the result. The case which I have described, whose limb I saw severed from his body, survived for several days. Every day I would carry to him a cup of buttermilk & he would express such gratitude, for he could not eat any thing & he subsisted on what I brought him & a little loaf of bread. He never seemed to have recovered from the effects of the chloroform—His eyes ever have a sleepy, drowsy expression. He was as patient as a Lamb, for he was a child of God. Day after day he lay upon his back, troubled & perplexed by the swarming flies, disturbed by the bursting shells. Gradually he sunk—grows weaker & paler, until he found relief from all his pain in the sweet sleep of death. I have described this case because it represents the condition of hundreds & their sad end.

Poor Captain Coopwood! His end is drawing nigh. Ever since he received his awful wound he has been willing to converse upon the subject of religion. I talked with him freely & he seemed desirous to place his thoughts upon the future & endeavor to make some preparation. But his pain was so great—his body so restless & his mind so confused that he often complained that he could not collect his thoughts & place them upon any subject. I exhorted him to look to Christ & trust in him. Said he, 'Parson, my mind is too weak'. What a poor chance has the unpardoned sinner to make his peace with God when death is staring him in the face. His mind is confused—he is filled with terror—there is so much to do & so little time remaining /p. 39/ that the mind shrinks back from the task. How few ever make their peace with God in their dying moments. As yet the Captain had entertained some hope of recovering. One morning I called in to see him & saw a great change had come over his face. His pulse was fluttering fast. Mortification had begun & was progressing rapidly. He felt the change. He called me close to his side & told me his fears & requested me to ask his doctor if there was any chance for him. I did so & was told there was no hope in his case. I went back to the Captain with a sad heart, afraid almost to tell what was the opinion of the Physician. But upon his request I informed him that he must die & watched closely his contenance. He was not surprised for he had already felt the approach of death. O What a moment that must be when the truth flashes across the sinners mind that he must soon stand before his God. During all this day & the coming night he was suffering intensely. He said to me: 'I am passing away'. He would use the same expression to his friends around, 'I am passing away'. He then pointed to his servant who had been faithfully watching by his bedside day & night. I turned around & the tears were streaming from the boys eyes, running down upon his cheeks & falling to the ground. He sobbed like a child. No doubt he loved his master. The Captain said he hoped that his sins were forgiven. He now said 'O that I could now go'. In a few minutes after he closed his eyes in death.[41] /p. 40/

I will mention another case which to me was deeply interesting. You remember that I noticed a large, stout, young man who was wounded in the breast. His wound at first was regarded as very dangerous if not mortally wounded. I had passed him several times but had not as yet spoken to him. He found out by enquiring that I was a Chaplain & he sent me word that he wished [me] to converse with him. I readily consented & found him very serious & determined to seek the Lord whether he recov[er]ed or whether he died. He did not seem to think that he would die. He would request me to pray for him, saying that he had been a very wicked man & that he had a praying father & mother in Texas (for he was a Texan & a Lieut.—in Walls Legion).[42] Every time I returned to see him he would enquire of me if I had been praying for him. For some time he seemed to be doing very well & strong hopes for his recovery were entertained. But one morning when I called as usual to see him his pulse was very much excited & his heart was bounding & leaping as if it would break through its prison. His breathing was very difficult. His fate was sealed—inflammation had begun & he cannot survive but a few days. I enquired of him how he was progressing in making his peace with God. 'O, said he, I am making no progress at all. I feel no better'—Then he would close his eyes & pray. Deeply did I sympathize with him for I knew he had but a short time to live—But all I could do was to commend his soul to the /p. 41/ mercy of God. In the coming night he sent for me. As soon as I saw him I discovered a great change in his countenance—his face was radiant with joy—his eyes beamed with delight & a sweet smile was upon his lips. He caught me by the hand & said he had made his peace with God. That he was happy in the Lord. He then requested me to pray with him. During the exercise he was deeply engaged & expressed great delight. Then he called up some of his men & said to them—'You have now seen what we have been doing When you write to my Father & Mother tell them what your eyes have seen & how I died rejoicing in the Lord'. I remained near him all night—slept in hearing distance at his request. The next morning he was still rejoicing & gave every evidence of being a converted man. He died during the day. I trust in the triumps of the faith of Christ. No doubt the prayers of a pious father & mother were heard in his salvation though they were far away & he died in battle—How would their hearts rejoice to hear that their dying son had laid hold upon Christ in his last moments.

O the sufferings of the wounded! The whole air in
the tents was contaminated. It sickened the heart & the
body to pass amongst them. There lies one who had been
mortally wounded—shot through the middle of his body.
His wound is awfully offensive. The flies swarm around
him—He tears the bandage off. The vile worms crawl in
& out of his body. There is no hope for him. His wounds
are not dressed—At last death comes to his relief. He was
a Catholic but /p.42/ said that all his trust was in Christ.
There was another case that made me miserable every
time I saw him. It was that young man that was shot
through the ear, the ball passing down through his shoulder & lodging down deep into his body. His wound was
fatal, but O how his soul lingered in his suffering body.
He was so restless—he would not allow a sheet to stay
over his shoulder—nor a bandage upon it. The flies
would swarm upon him like bees upon a hive. His wound
was filled with insects. Still he could not die. I gave him
all the advice I could. Every day I hoped that death would
relieve him of all his pain. Day after day he lingered out
his weary life—Until at last after untold horrors the
friendly hand of death stopped his anguish. Pen can never
tell the misery & agony of the wounded soldier in these
cheerless hospitals. Those who live must lie for weeks
upon their backs; or their sides without changing their positions. Besides all this the mortar shells were bursting all
around them—sometimes pieces flying so near them as to
unstring their nerves. They have felt those awful shells &
they dread them the more. At night they have no rest for
the air above them is almost always filled with a rushing,
exploding bomb. If they should happen to fall asleep, they
are soon aroused by the crashing sound. Sweet sleep is
kept far from their eyes. In the morning they wake up
from such disturbed slumbers, unrefreshed & feverish to
spend a restless day amidst the heat & swarming flies.
/p.43/ In the morning their prayer is, 'Would to God it
were even' & when the evening comes, 'Would to God it
were morning'. Said one to me who had his hand torn all
to pieces by a shell & his whole arm swollen & inflamed

up to his shoulder 'O, have I to suffer here all day—must I lie here in this distress all the live-long day'. Here we see the need of Christian patience & fortitude. What is there in this awful condition to sustain the heart of the wicked man? Here we see the horrors of war—The cruelty of this barbarous evil! O Liberty how precious & costly is thy price! Thus has it ever been. For this precious boon the best blood must be shed & untold sufferings endured. When the battle is fought we rejoice in the victory but we are too apt to forget the anguish & suffering of the wounded. How much better to perish at once on the battle field than to linger out a miserable life for days after receiving a mortal wound. During this week our wounded men died rapidly—four or five every day at this hospital. Wrapped up in their blankets & placed in very inferior boxes they would be placed in shallow graves in the adjoining hollow. Sometimes the name would be marked— sometimes only a rude board & a small mound of earth would tell the spot where the unknown dead lie. Though no tear is then shed over the grave, yet far away hearts will bleed & tears will flow from the eyes of mothers & sisters & wives for those who lie sleeping in this valley— unnoticed unhonored & unsung. For every grave shall make some heart desolate. /p. 44/

It was during this week that the first courier from Gen. Johnson reached our lines, after much difficulty & danger. He came down the Yazoo in a small canoe—then down the Mississippi river—having been fired upon frequently. He brought the intelligence that Gen. Johnson was organizing an army at Canton & that he would soon come to our relief.[43] This news was extended down the whole lines by order of Gen. Pemberton. How it cheered the hearts of our brave soldiers. Already were they encouraged & greatly lifted up by their repeated victories over the assaulting enemy. Now they felt that deliverance was at hand. That in a few days the thunder of Johnsons cannon would be heard in the rear & that with a strong force he would break the lines of the investing foe. No one now doubted but that Vicksburg would be successfully defended.

The rations of our men were now greatly shortened
—in fact reduced to one fourth. Still they bore it cheer-
fully, but complained of great weakness. Their rations was
cooked by a detail & sent up to them in the trenches.
Day & night they must lie cramped up in the ditches—
drenched at times with rain—remaining wet until dried
by the sun—then exposed to the hot rays of a burning
sun. Towards the end of this week, such hardships & exposure & the scanty diet began to tell upon our garrison
—The cheeks become thin—the eyes hollow & the flesh
began to disappear from the body & limbs—the whole
appearance was haggard & care-worn. Yet they were
cheerful and did not complain. /p. 45/ A few of them at a
time were allowed to retire in the valley behind the lines
& rest awhile—But it was but poor resting, for the shells
& minnie balls were as dangerous here as in the trenches.
Many of them prefered lying in their places in the ditches.
Some would read their Testaments—Others would sleep
half the day.—Thus would they quietly pass their time
while the storm of war was raging over their heads & the
broken tempest was falling all around & about them.
Now the monotony of the scene would be rudely broken
by the sudden [death][44] of one of their comrades—or a
fearful wound inflicted by a bursting shell. They were
restrained from firing & the enemy daily drew nearer to
our lines.

Third Week—[45] The mortar shelling this week was
most terriffic. Hospital No. 1 where the most of the
wounded of our Regt. were carried was most unfortunately located. It was in reach of the fire from the lines &
was about the limit of the range of the mortar shells from
the river. A negro while nursing was shot down by a
minnie ball in the act of waiting upon the wounded. One
of the wounded was also hit by the same kind of missile
while lying on his bunk. Fortunately the ball was too
much spent to do much damage. The house on top of the
hill where were the sick & some of the wounded also &
where the cooking was done & where we all took our
meals, was struck /p. 46/ several times by canon shot &

shell from the line. While at dinner one struck the house & exploded tearing down a large portion of the brick wall. A sick man had just risen from his bunk to look out the window. He left his watch & coat where he was lying. The coat was torn to pieces & the watch broken into a thousand fragments. Was not there a special Providence in this? Another shot passed through the house, barely missing two of the doctors while they were dressing— passed through two of the walls of the building & finally inflicted a mortal wound upon a poor fellow who was just recovering from a long spell of sickness. His hip was torn to pieces & he died the next day. While we were at break- fast one morning a shell just passed over our heads, hit a few steps in front of us, buried itself in the ground & then exploded scattering the dirt all around. We eat our meal more rapidly after this & sought the valley below.— Every time we eat our meals these shells from the line would trouble us—Also those monsters from the mortars —Scant as were our rations we could not eat them in peace.

Eight mortar guns were now playing upon the town & vicinity. Two of them ranged directly at our Hospital. I don't suppose they could see the yellow flag—If they could they seemed to have aimed at it. O how annoying they were to all especially to our wounded. Day & night they keep these poor suffering men in /p.47/ dread. At night the firing increases. They burst above the valley & send their howling fragments in the vale below & in the very midst of our wounded. Now a large piece falls in the tent & strikes in the street between the bunks, so that none are hurt but all are made uneasy. Now one hits the bunk upon which a wounded soldier lies & tears it down to the ground. Another piece falls through the tent strikes the ground near by & bounces upon the pillow where one is lying. They come rushing overhead—every one appearing as if they would fall right upon your head. Thus day after day our wounded as well as others were tormented by these missiles of destruction. They could not sleep at night—were always in dread. No wonder under such circumstances that they did not recover fast &

that many died. For sweet refreshing sleep had no sooner closed their eyelids, but some thundering shell would explode above their heads & drive slumber far from their weary eyes. The well & sound could not sleep with unbroken slumber—but would be awakened out of a sound sleep a dozen times during the night by these unwelcome messengers. None who lie down a night had any assurance but that before the day should dawn his body would be torn in pieces by a fragment of shell. /p. 48/

There was two nights during this week that I can never forget. The firing from the mortars was more frequent & nearly every shot exploded above us & around us. Lieut. Owen of our Regt.[46] was wounded & had come to this hospital for treatment. We slept together on the side of a steep hill in the valley, but had no care or any protection beside the position. The doctors had now left their rooms & had caves to which they would resort when not on duty. Our position was exposed also to the fire from the lines & we were on the wrong side of the hill for protection from that source—so when the firing from the mortars would slacken & that from the lines would increase we would change our position to the opposite side of the valley. Then again the mortars would become more furious & we would rather risk the firing from the lines. Solid shot from the lines would strike against the hillside above our heads & the large mortar shells burst above throwing their fragments all about us. At night we would watch the flying meteors & when one would seem to be making the descent right on our heads

we would shelter as close as possible to the side of the
hill. We would lie down to sleep & by the time that sweet
slumber began to close our eyelids, our nerves would be
shaken by a tremendous crash near our ears, which would
dissipate all sleep for a while. Then again composing our-
selves we would again fall off into a doze, only to be disturbed again by the same unwelcome sound. At midnight
when the whole world is wrapped /p. 49/ in forgetfullness
we were scarred frightened in our dreams & disturbed in
our slumbers. All we could do was to commit our souls
into the hand of Him that never sleepeth & who is able
to save from death. One night the firing was so hot I
thought I would try a cave in the hollow beyond us. So
into it I went before sunset. It had been a vacant one & I
thought I would have it all to myself. I moved my blankets
over & congratulated myself—upon having a good nights
repose—I felt more secure from danger. When night came
here comes two or three men—soon after a few more—
until the cave is crowded full. I thought I could still stand
it & remained quiet for some time. The shells were raging
over us & would sometimes strike so near us that we
would entertain some fear that our cave might be crushed
in by the falling of an unexploded mortar shell. After a
while the place became so hot & so crowded & the mos-
quitoes so bad—that I determined to leave & seek my
same old place where at least I could have air & room. So
I took up my bed, & over the hill went my steps increas-
ing in length & rapidity as some howling shell would
seem to pursue me. That was the only night I ever tried a
cave & I was satisfied with the open air afterwards.

Near our Hospital in the same valley was a large
cave with two or three families occupying it. They had
several children & could with difficulty keep them within.
Some of the little /p. 50/ fellows would crawl out & go to
playing on the green grass, until a shell would explode
near by when they would go rushing back again. An old
woman, who was their grandmother, was very much an-
noyed at the conduct of the children & would be always
calling them in. She seems to have had a perfect horror of
a shell. When the firing would subside, she would venture

out, but as soon as a shell came in a quarter of a mile, she would run back to her hiding place. They had their cooking done at their houses & their meals brought to them. They became exceedingly wearied with their cramped position & wished the siege would close in some way.

Our eating at the hospital this week was very scant. At first we had a plenty of bread & beef. Now we were allowanced to a small piece of beef & pea bread. The pea bread was made of peas & corn ground up together & mixed in about equal proportions. It presented a black, dirty appearance & was most unwholesome—as heavy as lead & most indigestible. But we did not have enough of this. We were thus kept half hungry all the time—consequently not in the best humor. But we fared better than our poor soldiers in the ditches. There were several orchards around & the apples about half grown. The trees were soon stripped of their premature fruit—even soldiers from the lines came out to share in the treat. The doctors at the hospitals lived like kings. There was no famine /p. 51/ to them. Their tables groaned with luxury & every abundance. Though Dr. Minor,[47] the Surgeon in charge, was a graduate of the same College & from the same State, & was acquainted with my brothers & had been at my Fathers house & seemed to be very friendly, yet it was never convenient for him to ask me to take a meal at his table, when he knew that my fare was miserably rough & short. Not withstanding my position as Chaplain,[48] he sent me to the same table with the nurses,[49] were it was a rush to procure what little we obtained & when not wishing to rush like a dog for my food—I requested of him that he would allow his servant to give me my portion to myself—even this boon was denied me—And for my miserable fare I paid one dollar per day. But as yet I could not help the matter—my duty was there with our wounded & there I must remain.

The hospital continued to be so much exposed that the physicians were talking about moving it to some more secure location. But it was a serious job & they dreaded it & about this time the firing was not so dangerous & they abandoned the idea. But they had long since refused to receive any more wounded & they sent off a great many of the sick. About this time the mortars ceased firing altogether. What was the matter? Some said that our men had went over at night & had silenced them. Others thought that they had gone up the river to drive Gen. Price out of Helena, for it was reported that he held that place.[50] /p. 52/ All kind of rumors now floated amongst the garrison. We heard that Gen. Price had captured Helena & had taken several gunboats & that he had turned all the guns toward the river so that no transport could pass. This report was generally credited, so our spirits were greatly raised & we thought that Grant[51] would be made to feel the pangs of hunger & would suffer the fate to which he had doomed us. The silence of the mortar boats at this time confirmed our minds in such a belief. We also heard that Gen. Lee had again defeated Meade & had demolished his entire army—That he held Arlington Heights & was shelling the City of Washington after having demanded a surrender.[52] This intelligence was said to have been received from a Northern Paper. This however was not generally credited, though all believed that Meades army had met with a great defeat. These rumors for awhile cheered the heart—We felt more confident of success. Besides couriers would come in, stating that Johnson had an army of ninety thousand men, that they had organized & were coming to our relief—that he would attack the rear of the enemy in ten days at most. Some said they could hear his canon in the rear. Again during this week the enemy opened a grand general fire of artillery as they did before—in order to intimidate our men & annoy them as much as possible. About three hundred pieces of canon were fired & loaded as fast as possible. The whole air was again filled with burning fuses & exploding shells. Our canon dared not open their mouths, but hid themselves /p. 53/ amid the embankments & hills. Even then—they were sometimes dismounted & torn to pieces—their casons exploded & their men killed. The breastworks were in places torn down & many of our brave men had seen their last day. But compared with the fierceness of the fire but few comparatively were killed. Our hospital building was shot through & through & the

hill was for a while cleared of its occupants—for all those
who were badly sick were removed & those who were
able to walk, sought shelter in the valley below. Solid
shot & shell would fall in the tents among our wounded,
but they seem to have been defended by the hand of God.
Thousands of these missiles would pass over & fall on the
city. All who had caves sought protection. Mules horses
& cows were killed on the surrounding hills. This heavy
firing lasted for more than an hour & then subsided to
the usual firing, the continual sharpshooting & the occa-
sional booming of the batteries.

Another week draws to a close[53] & no relief from
Johnson. Our men are weak from constant fasting & long
continued confinement. Some become disheartened &
begin to fear that Johnson will not come at all. The question with all is, How long will our rations last. Some say
not more than another week. Then we hear there is
enough to hold out to the fourth of July. All hope now
was from without. There was no doubt that our rations
were quite limited. The more hopeful still look for assistance as confidently as ever. /p. 54/

4th Week—[54] Owing to the silence of the mortar
boats the people of town, the wounded at the hospitals
and all the attendants felt great relief. The caves were
deserted in town—Women & children came out with joy
& entered again their pleasant rooms. The streets were
filled with citizens. The whole town seemed to breathe
freer. Now one could see ladies walking the streets at
their leisure—not with the hurried, uneasy step that
mared their gait during the bombardment. What a blessing
to walk the pretty streets of the city of hills without hearing the rushing of shells or the singing of flying fragments.
But alas! this quiet did not last long. Afar off in the distance from the same fatal spot, across the peninsula, a
cloud of white smoke rises up. Then the dull heavy sound
is heard—a sound too familiar to our ears—now comes
the rushing shell—high up in the air it explodes & sends
its whirling pieces all around. Before this unwelcome
noise has died out into the distance, another cloud arises
& here comes another unwelcome visitor—And then an-

other follows in quick succession. The mortar boats after a silence of one or two days have again opened upon the devoted city. What a bustle among the people. What a confusion in the streets. Mothers send for their children. They prepare to leave their comfortable houses. Everyone walks with a quick & hurried step. The courier puts spurs to his horse & flies with speed upon his errand. The teamsters put their horses into a quick trot & seek refuge behind the steep hills. The streets are soon cleared. The same feeling of /p.55/ dread & suspense settles down upon the mind. I happened to be in the town when the firing began & was deeply impressed with the change that came over the city. All our hopes were dissipated—the mortars had not left—neither have they been silenced. They had only ceased for the want of ammunition—now they had a new supply. Farewell then quiet peaceful moments—adieu happy hours of unbroken sleep. Ye wounded suffering men open now your eyes & ears in dread suspense. Sleep no longer with sweet slumbers during the long watches of the night. Again you shall be scarred in your dreams & frightened in your slumbers. Your eyes shall now remain open & wakeful & your weary limbs become doubly fatigued while you drag your burdened existence through long & tiresome nights, listening to the bursting bombs & for flying fragments as they fall around you, above you & near your miserable couch.

They seem to fire those mortars more rapidly than ever. One day I was standing upon the portico of the second story of the hospital building, watching the firing around the lines & enjoying the beautiful scenery that was spread out before me—for it was a high commanding point & overlooked the whole city, as well as part of our lines. While I was thus employed, enjoying the wide extended view & the cool refreshing breezes, one of those mortar shells exploded in front of me, high up in the air & sent one of the large fragments with singing, silvery sound right towards the building. /p.56/ It descended close to the porch in which I was standing & struck the ground near the steps with great force, tearing up the

yard at a fearful rate & filling the second floor with dirt
& sand. One of the sick men, a pale, slender fellow, was
just going out to get a drink of water. He was knocked
prostrate on the ground, almost covered up in dirt—we
thought he was torn all to pieces. No doubt he thought
the same, for he lay there some time. Feeling no pain, he
at last concluded that he would rise up. He stood upon
his feet—shook the earth from his clothes, surveyed his
whole person & then proceeded on quietly to the well,
where he had started to get a drink of water, as if nothing
had happened to him. This incident disturbed my pleasant
reverie & I preferred not to remain any longer in that
porch—as beautiful as the scenery was & as refreshing as
was the breeze.

Again Lt. Brack[55] & myself were reclining on the
side of the hill watching & dreading those mortar shells.
Here comes one making its path directly towards us—it
explodes in a dangerous position. We get as near as possible to a large apple tree near us & await the result.
Here comes one of the fragments. It threatens to fall upon
our defenseless heads—But the shield of God warded it off
& it falls to our side but two or three steps from us &
throws the dirt all over us. The piece would weigh twenty
pounds, tearing up a large hole & burying itself more
than two feet in the earth. This shocked our nerves con-
siderably. We felt thankful for our deliverance.

As soon as Lt. Brack had recovered from his wound
/p. 57/ I attended him part of the way to show him the
best route to the lines. The shelling from the river was
very severe & we had to cross a place that was particularly
in their range. As we approached this place we discovered
that the ground was tore up in several places. One would
now explode to our left & one to our right. We could not
avoid watching their movements. Presently one comes
directly towards us & explodes at the most dangerous
position. We stop—We hold our breath in dread suspense
—Pieces fly & fall all around us. A large fragment falls a
few feet behind us in the very path in which we were
walking. Had we stopped three steps sooner we would

both certainly have been killed. 'But it is not in man that walketh to direct his steps.' Why did we not stop sooner? The hand of God controlled our steps & spared our lives.

The Sabbath again spreads its sweet soft light over the earth. All nature is calm & serene. The birds sing sweetly—the soft & gentle breeze rustles throught the green leaves. The blooming Spring has now merged into the gay & cheerful summer. But while all nature is quiet & beautiful & refreshing, wicked man converts this paradise into a place of torment & evil. On this holy Sabbath there is no rest but war, with all its horrors, is desecrating its peaceful hours. No church bell chimes with silver tone, inviting careworn men to the worship of the living God. The air is filled with the crashing sound of the bursting shell—Nor can one in the shining morning or in the dying light of the declining evening retire to some /p. 58/ unmolested spot to hold sweet communion with God. Everywhere the missiles of death are flying around. His devotions are disturbed—broken up—By the time he confines his mind upon some consoling passage in the word of God, a thirteen inch shell explodes so near as to divert his attention & dispel all calm reflection. That calmness & serenity of mind which is so essential for the enjoyment of religious emotion is destroyed by anxiety, suspense & confusion. Often have I opened my little Testament & tried in vain to read a chapter with proper feeling. Again & again would I reprove myself for such a confused state of thought, reasoning with myself that my life was in the hands of God & that he could protect me at all times. Then I would resolve not to regard the danger, but soon a singing fragment of shell striking on the hillside near-by would dispel my good resolutions & disturb my thoughts. A time of danger is not favorable for religious emotions—though one is most solemnly impressed with the frailty of man & his dependence on God.

Since our hospital had now ceased to receive any more wounded & had sent the sick to the Washington Hotel a new hospital opened in town near the River & since the most of our wounded at Hos. No. 1[56] had either recovered almost or had died, I concluded that I would be more convenient to our wounded at other hospitals if I could get lodging in town. Besides the doctors were talking continually to move this hospital to a more secure place. In addition to this I did not think I was rightly treated here. Under these circumstances /p. 59/ I went in search of a new location. I had ascertained that Dr. R. H. Whitfield[57] had charge of the newly opened hospital at the Washington Hotel. There I went—Dr. W. kindly offered me a place in his own room & invited me to a seat at his own table. To me the change was delightful. Here we had a plenty to eat & I was compelled to watch my appetite closely, not satisfying it fully for two or three days. I eat about what I thought a decent man ought to & often ceased with as keen an appetite as when I began. In a few days all was right. The change of board restored my system. I recovered from my puny spell & began to strengthen every day. Here I could have retirement—was more convenient to the wounded & sick of our Regiment. Besides it was comparatively secure from those troublesome mortar shells—for the most of them passed over & it was too far from our lines to be disturbed by firing from that direction. I had a good bed, a chair to sit in, a table to write on—Had it not now been for these conveniences I would not now had the pleasure of writing you this letter.[58] This hospital contained the sick from the whole army. Besides the large hotel it comprises three other large buildings. Dr. W. with several assistants attended to the invalids. All the rooms were soon crowded with the sick & the dying— Some in bunks & some upon the floor. Everything was conducted as well as possible but O the horrors of a hospital! /p. 60/

On the lines there is no change. The firing continues incessant. Their sharpshooters approach nearer, until they entrench themselves under our very works. They continue to pour a perfect stream of minnie balls over the heads of our men. One cannot raise his head above the parapet without endangering his life. A hat is placed on a gun stick & raised up in a few minutes it is pierced by half a dozen balls. One cannot rise to adjust his blankets or relieve his cramped limbs without great risk. Our men for a

THE WASHINGTON HOTEL HOSPITAL
*"Here I could have retirement.... I had a good bed,
a chair to sit in, a table to write on—Had it not been
for these conveniences I would not now [have] had the
pleasure of writing you this letter."*

pastime dig small excavations in the ditches which affords
protection from an enfilading fire. Some cut portholes
through the breast-works & through these small holes
fire upon the enemy. About this time we planted a mortar
in one of the valleys behind our works. Now we open a
fire upon the enemy from this retired position. What a
terrible fuss this mortar produces amongst the enemy. It
does not fire more than two or three shots before it draws
down upon its devoted head the concentrated fire of all
the enemies available guns. The 40th Miss.[59] was in front
of this ill-fated mortar of ours. So severe was the fire that
our breastworks were leveled to the ground in places &
the regiment forced to retire for a while from the ditches.
Stop that old mortar was the command! The impudent
thing was commanded to close its mouth & to remain as
meek as a lamb. When this had ceased the enemy after in-
flicting what they thought a sufficient chastisement for
such presumption relaxed their fire & our retiring regiment again /p. 61/ took their places in the ditches. During
the night the works were repaired. Only now & then at
long intervals & very slyly would our old mortar dare to
open her mouth—though concealed deep in the valley
below. How long shall the endurance of our men be
tested? Who ever heard of men lying in ditches day &
night exposed to the burning sun & drenching rains for a
period of thirty days & that too under continual fire & on
quarter rations—Their limbs become stiff—their strength
is frittered away—Their flesh leaves their limbs & the
muscles relax & their eyes become hollow & their cheeks
sunken. Their clothes are covered with dirt & O horrible
their bodies are occupied by filthy vermin, the detestible
bodyguards. Thus were men of refinement & polish, in
the habits of preserving great external decency, subjected
to this deep & severe humiliation. Nor could this be
avoided, for the ditches were alive with these crawling
pests & to escape was impossible. This was not the least
of the many vexations with which the brave defenders of
our country were afflicted. Our men begin to show signs
of discouragement. They have waited for Johnson so long,
that hope defered makes the heart sick. Often they imag-

ine that they hear his canon in the rear. News is brought
in that he has crossed the Big-Black—that they had an
engagement with the enemy & defeated them. But so
many false reports have been circulated that our men are
slow to credit any.[60] It is now the middle of June & no
relief. The sanguine still hope /p.62/ while the desponding give up all hope.

5th Week—June 14-21.[61] This week passes away
without any particular variation. My duty calls me to visit
every day the wounded at the different hospitals. The
mortar shells fall in every part of town—in many places
depriving the suffering of what little repose they might
otherwise enjoy. At Hospital No. 1, my old home, the firing continues very dangerous. Well would it have been
for some had they have moved all the wounded to some
more secure place when they were speaking of it. Surely
they had sufficient warning. There are one or two cases
which I must here mention. At this hospital there was a
young man from some Louisiana Reg. that was dreadfully
wounded upon his shoulder by a shell. Nearly all of the
flesh from one of his shoulders, down towards his back
was removed. By the closest attention his life may be saved.
The Captain of the Company to which this young man
belonged happened to have his wife with him at the time
& she was a particular friend to the one who was wounded.
She attended him to the hospital & for several days did
not leave him day nor night. Then she made arrangements
to stay in town at night & return early every morning.
No matter how severe the shelling was, she came as regular as the rising of the sun, always bringing some good
nourishment for her friend. The wounded man improved
under this kind treatment. Often have I noticed this brave
woman make her visits at the peril of her life. She would
go when /p.63/ the shells were falling all around—when
the roads to town was literally torn up by them—when
even brave men would shrink from the danger. Thus
week after week, with untiring diligence would she nurse
& feed this young man. Now her cheek becomes pale
from constant labor & her strength evidently begins to

fail. About four weeks after the wound was inflicted a young man of the same company attends upon his wounded friend at night. He remains in the ditches during the day & at night he watches at the bed side of his wounded friend. On a certain night the firing from the mortar shells was furious. One bursts over head a large fragment passes through the tent & takes off this young mans head, while he was sitting up with his wounded friend. You remember the case of that young man who was wounded through the mouth & who bore his sufferings so patiently. When he was just beginning to recover, he changed his bed & one night on the fourth week of the siege, he was struck by a piece of shell on the thigh & a most dangerous if not mortal wound inflicted. How depressed he seemed—how hard he thought his lot was! Another young man at the same hospital (No. 1) was a nurse on account of being disabled by the loss of an arm. One day he was struck with a solid shot from the lines & his leg was amputated. Thus was he mutilated—a leg & an arm /p.64/ off from the same side. These sad casualties caused the doctors to move the hospital to some more secure place. They were all removed near the river to the Marine Hospital—Thus was our old hospital broken up—and well was it for our wounded that they were removed from where they were, for in two or three days after, the whole place was riddled with shells. The house was torn all to pieces. A pot was left behind & when it was sent for it was broken to atoms by a shell. The cooking house was almost demolished & the whole yard & the valleys below were ploughed up by the shells from the mortars & the lines. Some new batteries from the lines had been planted that played right upon this unfortunate location.

During this week—our hungry men could be seen walking the streets in search of something to eat. Some would buy sugar at an enormous price & walk along eating it from their hands without any bread. Molasses was ten dollars a gallon—flour five dollars a pound & meal one hundred & forty dollars per bushel & none to be had scarcely at that. The poor soldier does not meet with the cakes & pies which once filled every corner of the streets. All the eating houses are closed. The poor in town are upon the verge of starvation. Lean & haggard famine stands at the door of the rich & knocks for admission. All that our soldiers get for one day could be eaten at one meal & not /p.65/ be sufficient. Two common size biscuits, two rashers of bacon—a few peas & a spoon full of rice constitute one days allowance. The men are half hungry continually & do not feel in a good humor. All things go on as usual until Saturday the 20 of June. Early in the morning, before broad daylight I went down to the rivers edge to bathe. I went thus early because of the sharpshooters across the river who had for the past few days been firing upon our teamsters & had killed & wounded three or four. Hence I went to bathe before it was good daylight. While I was there enjoying myself in the cool & refreshing waters of the mighty river, a tremendous canonading opened along the whole line. It was certainly the heaviest that occurred during the siege for the enemy had been mounting new guns all the time. They had received & planted some heavy pieces & they opened upon us with all their might this morning as soon as they could see how to shoot. Some of their shot came clear across the whole town & fell half way across the River. They make a peculiar sound when they strike the water sounding more like they come in contact with a rock than with a yielding element. For two long hours they continued this awful fire. The gunboats below also joined the revelry. Surely they must be demolishing our works & killing our men at a fearful rate. Some thought they intended another charge But they had enough /p.66/ of charging & were content now to annoy our men by their artillery. As severe as this firing was & of as long continuance as it was but few of our men were hurt & but little damage was done to our works. If such a shelling as this could not drive our men from the trenches, they need not try any more—But some of our brave boys were sent to their long home, where they will never more hear the canons roar.

Sunday again comes.[62] Every morning I visit our sick

and wounded. At Lees Brigade Convalescent Hospital, there is preaching, every Sunday. The place was tolerably secure. This Sabbath I attend there & preach for them in the evening. There I went with seven Chaplains—three of whom were Baptists.

This week the enemy began to plant guns on the other side of the river. At first they fire a small movable cannon & change their position at every fire. Our old Columbiads[63] thunder at the little impudent thing. Here comes another shot from this small cannon & strikes on the street before you hear the sound. Our guns fire at the smoke—But no doubt the active thing is far away before this, for it seems to be drawn by horses. Thus they were trying our strength. After awhile they plant a heavier gun on the opposite bank, behind a mound. They open fire upon the town & make it dangerous to walk the streets. Our large guns open a furious fire upon /p.67/ this small gun. Old Whistling Dick[64] tries his skill also—But in vain. They cannot dismount it. Sometimes the shell would burst exactly over the spot & we would think that it was silenced, but after a while it would open again & send a defiant shot on Main Street again. Our guns seeing that they would not dismount it ceased firing except occasionally when the enemy would seem to be too saucy. The enemy encouraged by this effort went to work & mounted other guns, so that this part of town began to be quite dangerous.

This week Dr. Beaty[65] came to the same hospital. I secured for him a good room, telling Dr. W. that he was a particular friend of mine. He was not sick much but was afflicted with great nausea in the stomach. He could eat nothing scarcely. I was fortunate to find a nice family who gave me every morning a cup of milk—which was all the Dr. would eat during the day. Every day would this kind lady give me this portion of milk. Her daughters sometimes with their own hands would serve me. These ladies seemed to have been in good spirits & believed firmly that Johnson would come to our relief. The citizens generally, I think, were hopeful.

Thus passes the fifth week of the dreadful siege—No relief yet. Our men are discouraged, though some are yet hopeful. /p. 68/

Sixth and Seventh Weeks—[66] When will this long letter end. I must hurry to a conclusion. The enemy occupied about this time a high hill in front of Hubert Brigade[67] & planted there a heavy battery in fifty yards of our works. This they did to cover their mining operations. Now they begin to try the plan of undermining our works. Day & night they dig. Our men endeavor to countermine & each party can hear the clinking of the tools of each other. But our operations are not successful. The enemy push on the work with great energy—So close are the parties to each other that we throw hand grenades amongst them & sometimes they throw them back before they explode. Their ditches extend in twenty steps of our men. Gen. Hubert has a line constructed in the rear of our first works & seeing that the enemy will shortly blow up the fort, hill & all, he orders them to abandon the threatened line. Everything is now ready—The mine is finished—The time comes to touch the fatal match—They intend making a charge at the time of the explosion. Their men are all drawn up in readiness for that purpose. On the 25 of June they fire the fatal match. An awful explosion takes place. The hill is shaken as if by an earthquake. Louder than the thunders of heaven rolls on this mighty sound. It seems like the earth is moved—The hill is torn up, the fort is demolished & ruin is spread all around. Now they make another charge /p. 69/ before the clouds of dust & smoke disappear. The noble 3d Louisiana[68] receives it with their wonted courage. They drive back the foe with dreadful slaughter, sustaining a heavy loss themselves. Again they begin their mining operations, endeavoring to force our lines at this position. Like rats they work under the ground. They are checked at our countermining operations at times. Still they progress. On the 29, another mighty explosion takes place. At this time several of the brave 3d La. are killed & wounded. A mighty chasm is made in our lines & the enemy occupy the position which was once our lines. But they dare not show their heads above the embankment.[69]

"So close are the parties to each other that we throw hand grenades amongst them & sometimes they throw them back before they explode."

The firing from the other side of the river was now becoming furious. Heavy Parrot guns are planted on the Peninsular behind the solid banks. With what power & fury do they now send their shots through the very heart of town. It becomes now very dangerous to walk the streets. Our hospitals in town suffer. Here comes a furious shot, swift as the winged lightning, giving no time for dodging. It strikes a brick wall a few steps before—passes through two or three houses & then explodes. One entered the hospital where poor Bob Harold[70] was lying wounded. It explodes in a few feet of his head—tearing his head off & leaving nothing but his chin. I had conversed with him the evening before. He was /p.70/ so cheerful. Said he was enjoying religion more than he had for a long time. Was talking about his wife & how glad he would be to hear from her. The next day he was called from this world of trouble. Several ladies were killed & wounded from these Parrot shells across the river. While one was dressing in the morning, a shell entered her room, exploded—destroyed her bonnet-box but did not touch her, almost frightening her to death. The sharpshooters across the river keep up a fire at the teamsters that go to the river to water their stock & at those who come after barrels of water for our soldiers, for they hauled water to our lines. At twilight they would converse with our men across the river— 'How far is Johnson in the rear? We are coming over to see you on the 4th of July & to get dinner'. Some fellow replied 'You had better come pretty early in the morning, for we will eat all up pretty soon'—They would talk & joke every evening.

In town was a high hill,[71] on which a house was built & where our men were accustomed to watch the movements of the enemys boats in past days. It was occupied by a company of Engineers. There I would frequently go at sunset & take a view of the great river & the surrounding scenery. Often on Sunday evening would I wonder— What shall be the fate of this city & our army by the next coming Sabbath. One day the enemy /p.71/ opened fire upon Sky Parlor as it was called—for they had observed our men upon this point. Two was killed & three or four

wounded. This made us a little shy of this parlor of
natures.

As I was wallking down the river on a visit to the
Marine Hospital I saw several men cutting up & dressing
what I at first thought was beef. But near by I discovered
a head with long ears—a veritable mules head. It was
mule beef! This told a sad tale. Our provisions were running low.[72] The sixth week had now closed & nothing
from Johnson. Our fate seems to stare us in the face. Still
we hear rumors that he is coming with a mighty army. O
that we could hear his canon thundering in the rear!
What a welcome sound. Cant our government send us relief Shall Vicksburg fall for the want of energy on the part
of our government? Will all the blood shed be spilled in
vain? For the first time dark doubts would cross my
mind. Maybe Johnson cannot get sufficient troops to
come to our relief. Ever of a hopeful disposition, I would
not listen to such fears, but would still believe that at the
last hour, the long expected help will come. Visiting the
lines frequently, I discovered that the men generally had
almost given up hope of relief from without. They considered the place as lost, though they were willing to lie
in the trenches another month if it would save the place.
/p. 72/

On the 3d of July the firing begins to cease upon the
lines. What can be the matter? A flag of truce is sent in
from our General to the enemy. What is the meaning of
this? Great excitement prevails throughout the garrison.
Some suspect that a surrender of the town is in contem-
plation.[73] At such a thought the indignation is universal
& almost beyond control. Our brave men, who had endured so much from hunger, danger, exposure & fatigue
could not endure the thought of loosing all their labor.
The thought of yielding up their arms into the hands of a
hated foe & becoming prisoners of war was beyond endurance. To calm this excitement & give the men time
for sober second thought, so that mutiny & rebellion
might be avoided, the rumor was circulated that the flag
of truce was only to request permission for the removing
of some citizens out of the enemies lines. Now the ceasing

of the firing extends around the whole lines—Silence reigns
where but a few hours before the terrors of war were
furiously raging. The streams of minnie balls now cease.
The bursting shell is no longer heard. On the extreme
left, firing still goes on, for the intelligence had not reached
to that point. All now has stopped, except the mortar
guns & the Parrot canon that play upon the city. There is
peace on the lines but war in the city. In fact the firing
upon the town seems to increase in fury. New guns have
been planted on the opposite side of the river. In the afternoon, when the firing was somewhat subsided, I started
down to the Marine Hospital, which was down the river
more than half a /p.73/ mile. Just before I reach the
place, a powerful battery of Parrot guns open upon the
town & the range of their shot was between my position
& the hospital. O with what power would those furious
missiles come & strike the hills & roofs & walls of buildings. I watched the range of the shot for awhile & came
to the conclusion that it would be risking too much to
proceed. So I concluded to return & await a more favorable opportunity for my visit. As I was about to return,
other batteries opened upon the town & the mortars short-
ening their fuses, shelled the streets next [to] the river.
But the street on the rivers edge seemed to be safe
enough for one to walk without much danger—for the
shot & shell passed over. So I went down near the river
& with pretty quick step was making my way back. Our
large siege guns were replying most furiously. Gen. Pemberton, looking upon matters as desperate, had given the
order to return shot for shot with the enemy. So all of
our guns on the river replied rapidly. The firing was by
far the heaviest that had taken place on the river during the
siege. Our large Columbiads poured their rushing shell
over my head—the enemies shot in reply passed over.
The mighty river rolled the resounding thunder along. It
was fearfully sublime. With quick step I was making my
way up the river on the lower street, endeavoring as soon
as possible to pass this dreadful crossfire. The mortar
shells & shot generally passed over my head. Now one
explodes over the rivers edge—just in front of me /p.74/

in a most dangerous position for myself. I was aware of
my imminent peril. At the moment of the explosion, I
stopped—held my breath & waited—in awful suspense.
The result—Fragments fell all around me. One piece
came down near me & struck the ground in a few feet &
then rebounded & struck me in the side. It was a fragment from a large mortar shell, weighing more than one
pound. It came down in a line so perpendicular to the
earth, that it spent the most of its force upon the ground.
I could see the piece as it rebounded & endeavored to
evade it. It only stung my side without breaking the skin
or even bruising the place. I picked up the fragment &
went on my way rejoicing for this narrow escape—thank-
ing God that he had let me off with such a gentle stroke.
Others had been mangled & torn to pieces—some sent to
the grave, others disabled & maimed for life, but he smites
me so gently with his kind hand as to teach me my great
danger & to show me his protecting hand.

Just before I reached the hospital where I was residing—after having arrived safely out of the range of the
firing—I heard the shrill note of the artillery-man's
bugle. It was the first time I had heard the blast of the
bugle during the siege. In a moment our canon ceased firing. The enemy beyond the river also ceased & stillness
again rested upon the peaceful bosom of the father of
waters. Now for the first time for many long weeks, the
sound of canon is not heard. /p.75/ At three o clock in
the evening, Gen. Pemberton in person seeks an interview with Gen. Grant.[74] This looks very suspicious. I
visit the lines. The impression there prevails that a surrender will be made. Night approaches. All is still. The
morning dawns.[75] I arose by the dawn of day, I listen for
the usual sharpshooting—The crack of the rifle is not
heard. How glad would I have been to have heard once
more the booming of the canon—A sound once so annoying, yet now how welcome—For it would have told
the glad news that our devoted city had not yet been surrendered. But a painful silence, foreboding evil, reigns
over the doomed city. The bright sun rises. The sound of

*"Gen. Pemberton in person seeks an interview with
Gen. Grant."*

firearms is no more heard. Has a surrender been made? Hope that had so long lingered in my heart begins to take its flight. Darkness settles over my mind, As yet we in the city had not received any certain intelligence of the result though it was known on the lines & our noble men had already stacked their arms. They begin now to distribute clothing at the hospitals. In a short time, I hear the sound of horses feet clattering on the pavement. Upon looking up the street I beheld a sight that I fondly hoped never to see. A Yankee officer, in blue uniform, galloping down the streets of Vicksburg. This too on the 4th of July. Here comes those hateful gunboats. They can now pass our batteries with impunity. Poor Whistling Dick will never have the pleasure again of /p. 76/ sinking any of these monsters. As their gunboats come moving slowly up the river they fire the national salute—This sound fell most unwelcomely upon our sad ears. They now rejoice, while we weep & lament. At twelve o clock the sound of music greets our ears. Here comes the victorious army with flying banners & joyful music. They are covered with dust—for clouds of it rise as they march. They did not seem to exult much over our fall, for they knew that we surrendered to famine, not to them. The streets are now filled with their soldiers—They break open stores & closed houses & pillage & destroy the contents. Confederate writing paper is thrown into the streets & trodden underfoot as utterly worthless. Sugar, whiskey, fresh fruit in air-tight cans—are enjoyed in great abundance. They invite our men to share in the booty & they feel no reluctance in participating.[76] Now the steam[ers] come pouring down the river as by magic. Ten or twelve can be seen landing at the same time. In a short time they line the levee up & down the river for nearly a mile in distance. They are loaded down with provisions of every kind.

At the close of the day, I visit once more Sky-Parlor. How changed now the scene. Spread out before me are the splendid steamers of the enemy, exhibiting the riches & power of our strong & wealthy foe. As I looked upon the scene & reflected upon the mighty blow we had just

"the victorious army with flying banners & joyful music."

received[77]—upon a long & protracted war that now awaited us—upon /p.77/ the streams of blood yet to be shed—upon the future slaughter of our young men & the carnage & desolation & destruction which should sweep over our beloved South, as I thought upon these things, tears of bitter anguish fell from my eyes & a cloud of darkness & gloom settled upon my mind. Farewell ye mighty hills, upon whose rugged peaks I have often stood & with solemn awe admired & adored the power of the Almighty to whom belongs the strength of the hills. No more shall I roam over those lovely hills & deep valleys, for they are now in the possession of a hateful foe—desecrated by the vile footsteps of a heartless, cruel & unprincipled enemy, who comes with the felonious purpose of desolating our homes, of spreading the shadow of death over our happy firesides & of enslaving a free & noble people. And, thou great Father of Waters,[78] upon whose lovely banks I have stood as sentinel in the silent watches of the night, [look]ing with covert eyes across thy dim & dark waters for the approach of the enemies boats, No more shall I guard thy rolling waves nor walk up & down thy friendly banks. Thy proud waves, unguarded by Southerners, shall now roll on to the mighty ocean, upon no friendly errand for us, but bearing upon thy placid bosom the power & wrath of our deadly foes.

Now dearest One, I must close this long letter, the longest no doubt which you will ever receive from my pen. I have written it at broken intervals of time in the midst of other duties & /p.78/ many interruptions. It has been composed in the midst of danger, when I knew not but every page would be the last, while the large shell was passing overhead & the missiles of death were flying around. During our investment I have attempted to send you a letter by a Courier going—in order that your mind might not be disturbed with fears in regard to my safety. I have written only what happened under my observation & what I could gather from reliable sources. Since it was intended only for your eye, I have not been backward in mentioning incidents in which I was principally concerned. I have recorded the dangers to which I was exposed so that you might unite with me in graditude to the great God who had been a shield to me during this remarkable period of my life.

As a testimony of esteem & affection & tender conjugal love to the wife of my youth, with whom I have spent many glad & joyful days, I have written this hasty epistle. Now unto Him that loved us & washes us from our sins in His own blood, be glory & honor for ever & ever—

Your most affectionate Husband—

W. L. Foster—

NOTES

1   Mrs. William Lovelace Foster (Sarah Mildred Maxwell). The Fosters
     had been married almost seven years when this letter was written.
     It is important to note that Foster began writing his letter to his
     wife on June 20, 1863. His narrative, however, begins several
     weeks before the date of the letter. Thus, close attention must be
     given to time sequence and to dating events earlier than June 20.

2   On April 30, 1863, Brigadier General John A. McClernand's
     Corps of the Union Army, commanded by General Ulysses S.
     Grant, bypassed the Confederate batteries at Grand Gulf and crossed
     the Mississippi River, landing at Bruinsburg, about 8 miles to the
     south. McClernand's Corps then advanced toward the town of Port
     Gibson, located 30 miles south of Vicksburg and 6 miles from
     Grand Gulf, almost due east from Bruinsburg.

3   Confederate division, commanded by Major General John S. Bowen,
     elements of which had been involved in the defense of Grand Gulf
     on April 29, moved to intercept McClernand's advancing forces,
     resulting in the Battle of Port Gibson, on May 1, 1863.

4   Confederate brigade, commanded by Brigadier General John C.
     Moore. The 35th Mississippi Volunteer Infantry Regiment, of
     which William Lovelace Foster was chaplain, was a unit of Moore's
     Brigade.

5   While Bowen's men were moving southeast to Port Gibson in
     order to intercept the advancing Union forces, a Confederate
     brigade, commanded by Brigadier General William E. Baldwin,
     moved southward from its camp near Vicksburg, crossed the Big
     Black River, and hastened to Port Gibson in order to assist Bowen's
     Division. Arriving just before noon, on May 1, Baldwin's Brigade
     joined Bowen's Division at Port Gibson in its effort to stop the
     Union troops. The Confederate forces were so outnumbered, how-
     ever, that by the end of the day the tide of battle at Port Gibson
     turned against them, and both Bowen's and Baldwin's troops were
     forced to relinquish Port Gibson to the enemy and to withdraw
     northward. Baldwin's Brigade returned to Vicksburg, and, shortly
     afterwards, took up a position near Warrenton. Bowen's Division
     moved to Bovina Station, a point on the Vicksburg and Jackson
     Railroad, about 8 miles east of Vicksburg.

6   It is unlikely that elements of Bowen's Division passed the camps
     near Warrenton. From contemporary reports, it appears that the
     "worn down & exhausted" troops which passed the camps there
     were those of Baldwin's Brigade.

7   Having captured Port Gibson, the victorious Union Army made its way towards Edwards Station, lying on the Vicksburg and Jackson Railroad, east of Vicksburg and the Big Black River, and approximately 23 miles west of Jackson. A Confederate army commanded by General John C. Pemberton was located near Edwards Station. Before attacking Pemberton's army, however, Grant decided to capture Jackson, where a smaller Confederate force was located.

8   Encountering little resistance, Grant's army captured Jackson on May 14, 1863.

9   General Joseph E. Johnston, CSA, was placed in command of all Confederate troops in Mississippi on May 9, 1863. He arrived in Jackson on the night of May 12. Determining that the Confederate troops in Jackson were insufficient to defend the city against Grant's advancing army, he ordered its evacuation, with the result that it was easily captured by the Union Army on May 14.

10   Confederate divisions commanded by Major Generals Carter L. Stevenson and John S. Bowen.

11   Confederate division commanded by Major General William W. Loring.

12   Confederate division commanded by Major General John H. Forney. It consisted of two brigades. The first was commanded by Brig. General Louis Hebert; and the second by Brig. General John C. Moore. The 35th Mississippi was a regiment in Moore's Brigade.

13   Vicksburg.

14   The Battle of Baker's Creek, better known as Champion's Hill, took place on May 16. In severe fighting, the Confederate army under Pemberton attempted to halt the advance of Grant's army toward Vicksburg. The Confederates failed to stop the Union army at Baker's Creek, however, and were forced to retreat in the direction of Vicksburg, taking up a position on the Big Black River.

15   Second Lieutenant William B. Brack, Company F, 35th Mississippi Volunteers.

16   Lieutenant General John C. Pemberton, CSA, Commander of the Confederate army defending Vicksburg. Pemberton had been promoted to Lieutenant General in October 1862; and placed in command of the Confederate forces in Mississippi at that time. His rapid rise in rank did not seem justified; and for this reason he was unpopular; and many who served under him readily believed the worst about him.

17   May 17, 1863.

18   May 18, 1863. General Pemberton, rejecting the advice of his superior, General Johnston, to evacuate Vicksburg while there was still time to escape, prepared to receive the onslaught of Grant's advancing forces.

19   Point on the Yazoo River, northeast of Vicksburg, where the Confederates had established an artillery position to defend Vicksburg against an enemy attack from that direction.

20   General John C. Pemberton, CSA.

21   General Pemberton, a native of Pennsylvania, was often viewed with distrust by his subordinates and by some citizens of Vicksburg. Although there is no evidence questioning his loyalty to the Confederacy, he was not a popular general. Mrs. Emma Balfour, in her diary written during the siege, undoubtedly expressed the opinion of many when she wrote: "Gen. Pemberton has not the confidence of officers, people or men, judging from all I am compelled to see and hear." A member of Hebert's Brigade of Forney's Division, commenting after the war, observed that the rank and file Confederate soldiers were in the habit of "taking the measure of their officers," and that this often had much to do with the outcome of the battles they fought. He then went on to say that he doubted that the soldiers of Pemberton ever entered into battle with hope of success.

22   Grant's first major assault on the Confederate fortifications at Vicksburg took place on Tuesday afternoon, May 19. Although the Union forces attacked with great determination, they were met with heavy fire from the Confederates, and, unable to breach the Vicksburg works, were repulsed. Grant lost 1,000 men in this unsuccessful assault and found that the Confederates were now an unyielding army, thoroughly committed to the defense of Vicksburg.

23   After General Johnston's evacuation of Jackson on May 14 and his unsuccessful attempt to induce Pemberton to extricate himself from Vicksburg before he was completely encircled by Grant's army, he endeavored to gather together sufficient troops and supplies with which to attack Grant's army, and thus make it possible for Pemberton's army to escape from Vicksburg. However, additional Confederate troops were slow in coming and thus the hope which the besieged troops placed in Johnston was illusory. As early as June 15, Johnston wrote his superiors in Richmond, "I consider saving Vicksburg hopeless."

24   Captain Samuel R. Coopwood, Company G, 35th Mississippi Volunteer Infantry Regiment.

25   Company G, 35th Mississippi Volunteers, of which Foster was chaplain.

26   Alabama Regiment.

27   On May 22, Grant made his second attempt to capture Vicksburg by direct assault on the Confederate works. Although the Union attack was extensive and forcefully carried out, Grant learned to his bitter regret that he was unable to carry Vicksburg by storm. Suffering over 3,000 casualties, he decided not to attempt another assault, but to continue the siege until his opponents were forced into submission.

28   Major General John H. Forney's Division, of which Foster's unit, the 35th Mississippi Volunteers, was a regiment. The intensity of the fighting involving Moore's Brigade was dramatically recorded in the following passage, included in a dispatch written by General Forney on the evening of May 22, ''General Moore has repulsed the enemy again on his right. This has been the most severe fighting. The battery of the enemy has nearly demolished his works.''

29   General Joseph E. Johnston, CSA.

30   The editor is unable to identify ''Dr. C'' with certainty. It is possible that he may be the ''Dr. Confield'' referred to in a letter written by William L. Foster at Vicksburg, on February 28, 1863, the original of which is in the William Lovelace Foster Collection, Manuscripts Division, The Historic New Orleans Collection.

31   Captain Charles A. Neilson, 35th Mississippi Volunteers.

32   Captain Samuel R. Coopwood, Company G, 35th Mississippi Volunteers, wounded on May 20 by an artillery shell.

33   May 23, 1863.

34   May 24, 1863.

35   Monday, May 18-Sunday May 24, 1863.

36   General Joseph E. Johnston, CSA.

37   May 25-May 31, 1863.

38   Schooners, specially modified and strengthened so that huge mortars could be mounted on their forward decks. Each mortar was capable of firing a 13-inch projectile a distance of 3500 yards or more.

39   There are several good contemporary accounts of cave life during the siege of Vicksburg. One of the best is *My Cave Life in Vicksburg*, by Mary A. Loughborough. New York, 1864. The most graphic description of cave life during the siege was written by one who was not present at the time. It is contained in Mark Twain's *Life On the Mississippi.*

40   The Union gunboat, *Cincinnati*, sunk by the Vicksburg batteries on May 27, 1863.

41   Captain Samuel R. Coopwood, Company G, 35th Mississippi Volunteers, who was severely wounded on May 20 by an artillery shell. The contemporary roll of this company, covering the period February 28-June 30, 1863, notes that Captain Coopwood was "killed in action" on May 27, 1863.

42   Waul's Legion, which had been recruited in Texas by Colonel Thomas N. Waul.

43   On Thursday, May 28, General Johnston's courier arrived with an official dispatch for General Pemberton. Emma Balfour, who was allowed to see this dispatch, undoubtedly greatly distorting its contents, recorded in her diary: "Gen. Johnston with 30 thousand and Loring with 10,000 men were at Canton and Jackson, that Bragg is marching to our relief, that Lee had driven the Yankees across the Potomac and they had burned Long Bridge and were in possession of Arlington Heights, and in addition to this, he, the courier, brought us 18,000 rifle caps which we greatly need and says two million are on the way! You may judge we were excited. The first piece of news from the outside world we had in 10 days, was glorious."

44   Foster omitted a word at this point in his letter, and "death" has been selected as the word he most probably intended to include here.

45   Monday, June 1-Sunday, June 7, 1863.

46   First Lieutenant William B. Owings, Company F, 35th Mississippi Volunteers.

47   Dr. Philip Pendleton Barbour Minor (1828-1884), Surgeon, CSA. Dr. Minor was appointed from Alabama on December 4, 1862, and reported for duty in Vicksburg by Special Orders dated February 5, 1863. He appears in the *Register of the Officers and Students of the University of Alabama*, Tuscaloosa, in 1843.

48   The status of chaplains in both Confederate and Union armies was not clearly defined. The names of chaplains were listed on regimental rolls with those of staff officers, but they were not accorded traditional military rank. It was not unusual for chaplains to find themselves at the mercy of capricious commanding officers, and this caused much resentment on their part.

49   Nursing was generally performed by enlisted men, who were convalescent or invalid soldiers.

50   General Sterling Price, CSA, of Missouri, commanded a division in the Confederate District of Arkansas. Helena, Arkansas, had been captured by Union Forces in July, 1862, and it was still in their hands at this time. Therefore, rumors that Price had taken it were erroneous.

51   Major General Ulysses S. Grant, Commander of the Union army besieging Vicksburg.

52   Robert E. Lee, having invaded Pennsylvania, met a Union army under General George G. Meade at Gettysburg in one of the greatest battles of the Civil War, July 1-3, 1863. Exhausted by the battle, General Lee began to withdraw his army in the late afternoon of July 4, ultimately crossing the Potomac and returning to Virginia. It is one of the strange coincidences of history that Vicksburg surrendered on July 4, 1863, the same day Lee's defeated army began its withdrawal from Gettysburg. These two mortal blows marked the beginning of the end for the Confederacy, which entered upon an irreversible decline culminating in its defeat in the spring of 1865.

53   Sunday, June 7, 1863.

54   Monday, June 8-Sunday, June 14, 1863.

55   Second Lieutenant William B. Brack, Company F, 35th Mississippi Volunteers. A contemporary roll of the Regiment indicates that he was "wounded slightly" during the siege of Vicksburg.

56   Hospital No. 1, which figured prominently earlier in this letter, was located about a quarter of a mile behind the lines of the 35th Mississippi Regiment.

57 Dr. Richard H. Whitfield, Surgeon, CSA. He was appointed from Alabama.

58 William L. Foster's letter is dated "Vicksburg, Miss—June 20." He apparently began writing it shortly after he took up quarters in the Washington Hotel Hospital.

59 40th Mississippi Volunteer Infantry Regiment, Moore's Brigade, Forney's Division.

60 Rumors, circulating in Vicksburg at this time, that a Confederate army under General Johnston was coming to the relief of the beleaguered city were indeed false, and many soldiers wisely hesitated to believe them. As noted previously, on June 15, 1863, General Johnston considered the situation in Vicksburg hopeless.

61 Monday, June 15-Sunday, June 21, 1863.

62 June 21, 1863.

63 Large cannon of various caliber used extensively during the Civil War.

64 Rifled, 18-pounder cannon used by the Confederates in the defense of Vicksburg. It became famous among Union and Confederate soldiers and sailors because of the distinctive whistling sound caused by the projectiles which it fired.

65 Dr. Beaty's identity has not been established.

66 Monday, June 21-Sunday, July 5, 1863.

67 Hebert's Brigade, commanded by Brig. Gen. Louis Hebert of Louisiana, was one of the two brigades in Forney's Division.

68 The Third Louisiana Volunteer Infantry Regiment of Hebert's Brigade. An excellent history of this regiment was published shortly after the Civil War. It is *A Southern Record. A History of the Third Regiment Louisiana Infantry*, by William H. Tunnard.

69 Foster is incorrect in placing this explosion under the works of the Third Louisiana on June 29. It was not until early afternoon on July 1 that the enemy exploded its mine. Tunnard vividly describes the great explosion, in which several members of the Third Louisiana Regiment were killed and wounded, in the following passage: "July 1. At 2 P.M. the enemy exploded the mine beneath the works occupied by the Third Louisiana Infantry. A huge mass of earth suddenly flew upward with tremendous force and a terrible

explosion, then descended upon the gallant defenders, burying numbers beneath its falling fragments, bruising and mangling them horribly. It seemed as if all hell had suddenly yawned upon the devoted band and vomited forth in sulphurous fire and smoke upon them. The regiment at this time was supported by the First, Fifth and Sixth Missouri Infantry, upwards of a hundred of whom were killed and wounded. Others were shocked and bruised, but not sufficiently to more than paralyze them for a few moments. At first there was a general rush to escape the huge mass of descending earth. Then the survivors without halting to enquire who had fallen, hastened to the immense gap in the works to repel the anticipated assault. The enemy, taught by a dearly-bought experience, made no attempt to enter the opening, not daring to assault. An immense number of 12-pounder shells thrown from wooden mortars descended among the troops, doing fearful execution. The fire was tremendous, rapid and concentrated, yet there was no flinching among those brave Southerners.''

70   Private Robert J. Harrold, Company F, 35th Mississippi Volunteers. Contemporary rolls indicate that he was wounded at Vicksburg on June 24, and killed on July 2, 1863.

71   The "Sky Parlor" was one of the highest hills in Vicksburg. Located two blocks from the river, a driveway on one side and a steep flight of steps on the other led to the top, which served as a popular observation point for both civilians and soldiers from which to view movements of gunboats on the river and the shelling of the city.

72   There are numerous contemporary references to the eating of mule meat during the last stages of the siege of Vicksburg. Although a novel form of meat, fresh mule was undoubtedly welcomed by soldiers who were half starved from lack of provisions.

73   On July 3, 1863, Pemberton sent Major General Bowen, under a flag of truce, to General Grant in order to propose an armistice of several hours, during which he hoped they might arrange acceptable terms of surrender.

74   At 3:00 P.M. on July 3, Generals Pemberton and Grant met near an oak tree to discuss terms whereby Pemberton would surrender Vicksburg. At first General Grant demanded unconditional surrender, but Pemberton, realizing Grant's desire to have the surrender take place on the "Glorious Fourth," insisted on concessions if the Confederates were to surrender on that day. Although at first appearing reluctant to compromise, by 10:00 that night, Grant proposed surrender terms which were acceptable to Pemberton. The

primary concession which Grant made was that the Confederate troops would be paroled; and thus would not be sent to Northern prison camps. Arrangements were made for the surrender and for Union troops to enter Vicksburg at noon on the following day.

75   Saturday, July 4, 1863.

76   During the siege, the Confederate soldiers at Vicksburg developed a special hatred for the merchants of the city who profiteered mercilessly at their expense. A Louisiana soldier expressed their feeling well when he wrote: ''These bloodsuckers had the audacity to hold their goods at such prices that it was an utter impossibility to obtain anything from them. . . .Some of these, worse than villains refused to sell to the soldiers at any price. . . .'' Reduced to scanty rations and mule meat, one can hardly blame the defeated Confederate soldiers for sharing in the booty of their conquerors, and enjoying the foods and drink which had been so long denied them by the Vicksburg merchants.

77   When Vicksburg fell, Grant captured 31,600 prisoners, 172 cannon, and 6,000 small arms. This has been described as ''the greatest military haul ever made in the western hemisphere.''

78   The Mississippi River.

BIBLIOGRAPHY

American Heritage Publishing Company, Inc. *The American Heritage Picture History of the Civil War.* New York: American Heritage Publishing Company, Inc., 1960.

Balfour, Emily. *Diary of Emma Balfour.* [Vicksburg], 1979.

Boatner, Mark Mayo III. *The Civil War Dictionary.* New York: David McKay Company, Inc., 1959.

The Civil War Centennial Commission. *Facts About the Civil War.* Washington: 1959.

Clemens, Samuel L. [Mark Twain]. *Life On the Mississippi.* Boston: James R. Osgood and Co., 1883.

Everhart, William C. *Vicksburg National Military Park, Mississippi.* Washington, D.C.: Government Printing Office, 1954.

Footprints: Journal of the Fort Worth Genealogical Society, 14:4.

Foster, L.S. *Mississippi Baptist Preachers.* St. Louis, Mo.: National Baptist Publishing Company, 1895.

Geer, Walter. *Campaigns of the Civil War.* New York: Brentano's, 1926.

Horn, Stanley F. *The Army of Tennessee.* Norman, Okla.: University of Oklahoma Press, 1952.

Johnson, R.U., and Buel, C.C., eds. *Battles and Leaders of the Civil War . . . being for the most part contributions by Union and Confederate Officers.* New York: The Century Company, 1887-1888.

Jones, J.H. "The Rank and File at Vicksburg". *Publication of the Mississippi Historical Society,* 7:17-31.

Kountz, John S., comp. *Record of the Organizations Engaged in the Campaign, Siege, and Defense of Vicksburg.* Washington, D.C.: Government Printing Office, 1901.

Long, E.B., and Long, Barbara. *The Civil War Day by Day: An Almanac 1861-1865.* New York: Doubleday and Company, Inc., 1971.

Mitchell, Lt. Col. Joseph B. *Decisive Battles of the Civil War.* New York: G.P. Putnam's Sons, 1940.

Palmer, Thomas Waverly. *A Register of Officers and Students of the University of Alabama, 1831-1901.* Tuscaloosa: University of Alabama, 1901.

Texas Baptist Herald. 1869, November 3.

Tunnard, William H. *A Southern Record. A History of the Third Regiment Louisiana Infantry.* Baton Rouge: Privately published by the author, 1866.

Wakelyn, John L. *Biographical Dictionary of the Confederacy.* Edited by Frank E. Vandiver. Westport, Conn.: Greenwood Press, 1977.

Walker, Peter F. *Vicksburg: A People at War, 1860-1865.* Chapel Hill: The University of North Carolina Press, 1960.

The War of the Rebellion: A Compilation of the Official Records of the Union and Confederate Armies. 128 vols. Washington, D.C., 1880-1901.

Warner, Ezra J. *Generals in Blue: Lives of the Union Commanders.* Baton Rouge: Louisiana State University Press, 1964.

Warner, Ezra J. *Generals in Gray: Lives of the Confederate Commanders.* Baton Rouge: Louisiana State University Press, 1959.

Washington, D.C. National Archives. Record Group 109, "War Department Collection of Confederate Records". XI: Records Compiled by the U.S. War Department; Compiled Military Service Records, part I (Men who served in organizations connected with one of the Confederate States).

Washington, D.C. National Archives. Record Group 109, "War Department Collection of Confederate Records". XI: Records Compiled by the U.S. War Department; Compiled Military Service Records, part III (General and Staff Officer's Papers).

Wiley, Bell Irvin, and Milhollen, Hirst D. *They Who Fought Here.* New York: Bonanza Books, 1959.

THE WILLIAM LOVELACE FOSTER COLLECTION

1855-1970

The Manuscripts Division
The Historic New Orleans Collection

This extensive research collection consists of nine manuscript letters, written during the period 1855-1873, by Rev. William Lovelace Foster, CSA, and members of his family. Included among these letters is Foster's excellent seventy-nine page letter describing the siege and fall of Vicksburg; and three relatively brief ones written by him during the Civil War, one from Vicksburg in February, 1863, and two from points near Mobile, Alabama, in the spring of 1864. Also included in the collection are 52 manuscript sermons written by Foster, from 1855 to 1867. Eighteen sermons are of the Civil War period. Most of these were written near Mobile, Alabama, and Atlanta, Georgia, in 1864. Unfortunately, they make little or no mention of military matters or the momentous events taking place in the Confederacy when they were written. In addition to the original manuscripts contained in this collection there is an extensive body of research material on Rev. William Lovelace Foster, CSA, the Foster Family, and the Maxwell, Lovelace, and Blair Families. Most of this research was done by Ralph W. Pierson for Edwin Blair during the early 1960's. It consists of hundreds of pages of notes and correspondence, as well as numerous copies of wills, military, church, and census records, newspaper clippings, family history narratives, and a 319 page typewritten manuscript by Ralph W. Pierson, entitled *The Saga of John Foster, Thomas Maxwell, and Their Descendants.*

────────────────────────────────

Board of Directors

Benjamin W. Yancey, *President*

INDEX

ILLUSTRATION CREDITS

Detail of "View of the City of Vicksburg, Miss., before its Investment by General Grant and Admiral Porter," from a sketch by Francis B. Schell. 1863. *The Soldier in Our Civil War* (New York, 1885), vol. 2, pp. 106-107.
Courtesy the New Orleans Public Library.

front endpaper

"Vicksburg: The Warren County Courthouse," anon. 1860.
Courtesy the J. Mack Moore Collection, Old Court House Museum, Vicksburg.

frontispiece

"Map of the Mississippi River," adapted from maps contained in *Decisive Battles of the Civil War*, by Lt. Col. Joseph B. Mitchell (New York, 1955).
The Historic New Orleans Collection.

xiii

"Map of Grant's Vicksburg Campaign," adapted from General Topographical Map, Sheet XX, Plate CLV, Julius Bien Co. Lith., New York. *Atlas to Accompany the Official Records of the Union and Confederate Armies, 1861-1865* (Washington, D.C., 1891-1895).
The Historic New Orleans Collection.

xvii

Detail of "Siege of Vicksburg—Attacks on the Rebel Works on May 22," from a sketch by Francis B. Schell. 1863. *Frank Leslie's Illustrated Newspaper*, June 20, 1863.
The Historic New Orleans Collection.

xx

First page of William Lovelace Foster's letter.
The Historic New Orleans Collection.

xxvi

"Map of the Siege of Vicksburg," adapted from map contained in *Vicksburg: National Military Park, Mississippi*, by William C. Everhart, Washington, D.C. National Park Service (Washington, D.C., 1954).
The Historic New Orleans Collection.

4

"The Sharpshooter—killing his seventh man," by Alfred R. Waud. ca. 1860-65.
The Historic New Orleans Collection.

10

Director of Publications:
  Patricia Brady Schmit
Book design:
  Larry Stultz, The Designshop, Inc., New Orleans
Production supervision:
  Rosanne McCaffrey, The Historic New Orleans Collection
Printing and Binding:
  Rose Printing Company, Inc., Tallahassee, Florida
Binding: Smythsewn Drawn-on-Cover
Type Face: Garamond
Text Paper: 60# Rose Natural
Endleaf: 80# Volume Natural
Cover: Kivar 3-12pt Linen